Text by Craig Turp
Edited by Jeffery Pike
Photography: Gregory Wrona
Design: Roger Williams
Series Editor: Tony Halliday

Berlitz® POCKET
GUIDE

Romania

First Edition (2006)
Updated 2006

PHOTOGRAPHY CREDITS
All photography by Gregory Wrona except
Mary Evans Picture Library 17;
Bettmann/Corbis 19; Reuters/Corbis 20.
Cover photograph: Catherine Karnow/Corbis

CONTACTING THE EDITORS
Every effort has been made to provide accurate
information in this publication, but changes are
inevitable. The publisher cannot be responsible
for any resulting loss, inconvenience or injury.
We would appreciate it if readers called our
attention to any errors or outdated information
by contacting Berlitz Publishing, PO Box 7910,
London SE1 1WE, England.
Fax: (44) 20 7403 0290;
email: berlitz@apaguide.co.uk
www.berlitzpublishing.com

The Palace of
Parliament in
Bucharest
(page 29) is a
testament to
Communist
kitsch

Romania is not sho
of natural wonders
Bicaz Gorge in
Moldavia (page 72)
is one of the
most spectacular

The painted
monasteries
of Moldavia
(page 67) are
the country's
artistic jewel

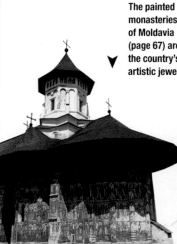

INTRODUCTION

Romania likes to market itself as 'always surprising' – and not without reason. It's a marvellous country, despite its own best efforts over the years to not be. Ruined almost entirely by war and socialism, it still has a long way to go before it becomes a full member of the European family, but progress is rapid. EU membership is on track for January 2007 – due more to political expediency than economic merit – though that will at least see the deregulation of the country's airspace and the coming of low-cost airlines. Until now Romania has been a cheap country to explore, though getting to it has often been expensive.

Is it worth the trip? Yes. Few countries in Europe still offer the old-fashioned thrill of travelling in the unknown. Much of Romania remains unexplored by visitors, and even the better-known towns and cities tend to be ignored. This is changing. The Ger-

> Romania has been the recognised international spelling of the country's name since 1974, when the United Nations agreed to change it from Rumania. The change came about after much lobbying from the Romanian government, which considered Rumania too Slavic.

mans spotted Romania's charms first, but now Brits and adventurous Americans are following in their tracks, with the monasteries of Moldavia and the mountains, medieval towns and castles of Southern Transylvania the most popular sights.

There is also a buzz about the Danube Delta: birdwatchers and nature-lovers have long known of its unique fauna and flora, and now non-experts are finding out what wonders there are in this isolated region. The Black Sea resort of Mamaia –

Bran Castle in Southern Transylvania, reputed home of Count Dracula

full of Western package holidaymakers in the 1970s and 1980s, deserted in the 1990s – is returning to former glory, though it is increasingly exclusive and expensive. Do not be fooled, however: Romania remains an off-the-beaten-track destination, and, although numbers of visitors will grow exponentially over the next few years, it will always remain refreshingly offbeat.

The Country and its Climate

Romania is the largest country in southeastern Europe, bordered to the north and northeast by the Ukraine and the Republic of Moldova, to the east by a short coastline along the Black Sea, to the south by the Danube and Bulgaria, and to the west by Serbia and the eternal rival, conqueror and enemy Hungary. Romania's area of 238,000 sq km (92,000 sq miles) makes it roughly twice the size of Great Britain. It is split into two by the Carpathian Mountains, which arch through the centre of the country. Mt Moldoveanu, which rises to 2,543m (8,343ft) almost in the exact geographical centre of the country, is Romania's highest mountain. Bucharest, the capital, where a tenth of the 22 million population lives, is in the far south of the country, on the Wallachian Plain, just 80km (50 miles) from the Danube and Bulgaria.

Romania has an extreme climate, with winters usually bitterly cold and summers stiflingly hot. Average temperatures in Bucharest in January range from -4°C to 2°C (25–36°F), while in August they usually climb well over 30°C (86°F). Precipitation levels all over the country are relatively low throughout the year, with the exception of the far southwestern corner, the area known as the Banat, where fierce downpours and flash flooding are common.

Landscape and Wildlife

Romania is blessed with a superb range of natural wonders, and despite the best efforts of the Communist central plan-

A BRIEF HISTORY

The first inhabitants of what is today Romania were almost certainly palaeolithic hunter-gatherers, attested by the remarkable dwellings found at Ripiceni, near Botoşani, and cave paintings at Cuciulat, in the county of Sălaj; both sites date from around 10,000BC. There is then something of a historical void until the first evidence of Thracian tribes appearing in the region, around 3,000BC, in the early Bronze Age. The Thracians were one of the original Indo-European tribes who populated vast swathes of Near Asia and Europe.

By 1,000BC the Thracians had devolved into smaller, more homogenous tribes, of which the Getae and Dacians (usually known collectively as the Geto-Dacians, and from around 100BC merely as the Dacians) were two of the most important. They inhabited the area between the northern Carpathians, the Danube and the Dniester. By

> The first mention of the Geto-Dacians in written history is by Herodotus, who tells us that, during the Persian expedition into Europe in 513BC, King Darius was 'resisted in Dobrogea by the Getae'.

the beginning of the 7th century BC the Greeks had established several colonies along the Black Sea. Relations with the Geto-Dacians were usually good, and the area prospered.

The Dacian State

Though the Scythians and Macedonians both made attempts to incorporate the Geto-Dacians into their empires, neither really succeeded, and by the time of Burebista, a Dacian king of the 1st century BC who united all Thracian tribes by fiercely resisting the Romans, we can talk of the existence of a genuine Dacian state. Ruling from Sarmizegetusa, near

A Getae royal helmet, now in the National History Museum

present-day Craiova, Burebista offered support to Pompey in his opposition to Julius Caesar, who, were it not for his murder, would have launched a full-scale invasion of Dacia.

Instead it was Emperor Trajan who finally invaded Dacia, almost 150 years later. The Roman victory was won in two campaigns (AD101–2 and 105–6) fought against Decebal, usually remembered as the greatest Dacian king. Dacia became a Roman province in 106, and officials, soldiers and merchants from all over the empire settled alongside the native Dacians. But the Romans did not stay long. When the empire went into decline, Dacia was almost the first province to be relinquished, abandoned to the barbarians by Aurelian in 271. Evidence of how deeply Roman culture penetrated the native Dacian culture during the 165-year occupation is today everywhere, notably in the Romanian language.

Hungarians and Turks

In the centuries that followed, Dacia was subjected to countless Barbarian invasions – Goths, Huns, Avars, Bulgars, Slavs, Pechenegs, Cumans and Magyars all blazed a trail across what is today Romania, leaving their mark and their genes.

By the beginning of the 13th century Transylvania had emerged as a relatively modern, well-run feudal principality firmly within the kingdom of Hungary. Indeed, two great men of Transylvania, Iancu de Hunedoara and his son Matei Corvin, ruled Hungary for much of the 15th century.

To the south, a defeat of Hungary by Wallachian prince Basarab at Posada in 1330 confirmed Wallachia as an independent principality. Basarab entered into pacts with Serb and Bulgar rulers to the east and south, and his son Nicolae Alexandru obtained the recognition of Byzantium.

In Moldavia it was a similar story. After a number of military victories against Hungarian forces, Prince Bogdan of Cuhea formalised Moldavian independence in 1359. In both Wallachia and Moldavia independence brought brief but rich periods of church and monastery building, and often a brutal implementation of the feudal system along Western European lines.

Then came the Ottomans. They first reached the Danube in 1395, but were defeated by Wallachian prince Mircea cel Batran (Mircea the Old). However, he could not resist them for ever, and accepted Turkish suzerainty in 1415, agreeing to pay a yearly tribute in exchange for relative independence. Moldavia, under the leadership of Alexandru cel Bun (Alexander the Good), held out longer, but after his death in 1432 it too had to succumb to Ottoman rule. In the 16th century, the Ottoman Empire expanded further. In 1541 Hungary was wiped off the map of Europe, and Transylvania, like Wallachia and Moldavia, became a pashalic of Turkey.

All three states remained firmly within the Ottoman sphere until the Turkish defeat at the Gates of Vienna in 1683 initiated the decline of the Sublime Porte's influence in Europe. Transylvania was restored to Hungarian, now Habsburg, rule in 1687, while Moldavia and Wallachia became increasingly difficult for the Turks to control. They responded by installing Greek phanariots to rule in their stead, no longer trusting local princes. Though the phanariots initially set about reforming the principalities, developing commerce, agriculture and general administration, they quickly became appalling rulers, who heavily taxed the local noble and peasant populations. Transylvania, meanwhile, prospered under relatively enlightened Habsburg rule.

Independence and Unification

A revolt in 1821 led by Tudor Vladimirescu forced the Turks to restore the rule of native Romanian princes to the provinces of Wallachia and Moldavia. After the Russo-Turkish War of 1828–9 Wallachia and Moldavia became Russian protectorates, though they officially remained within the Ottoman Empire. In 1861, with Russia weakened by defeat in the Crimean War, the two provinces joined forces as the United Romanian Principalities, under prince Alexandru Cuza.

Romania's German Dynasty

Romania's first king since the Dacian times was in fact a German. Karl Hohenzollern-Sigmaringen, a Prussian aristocrat, was offered the throne after the overthrow of Alexandru Cuza in 1866. Prince Karl's openly pro-German sentiments made him unpopular during the Franco-Prussian war of 1870–1, but his credit soared after the Siege of Pleven, which helped secure Romania's independence. As King Carol I (from 1881), he continued to support Germany and its ally Austria-Hungary, although his country was more sympathetic to France. Thus at the outbreak of World War I in 1914 Carol was unable to side with the Kaiser. Disappointed and thwarted, he died later that year in Peleş Castle, his splendid palace in Sinaia. He was succeeded by his nephew Ferdinand, and the Hohenzollerns continued to reign until 1947.

on 15 December, initially in protest at the demotion of a local priest. The demonstrations became political, and spread. Ceauşescu held a rally in Bucharest on 21 December to reassure the population that he was in control – but he wasn't. Despite much gunfire, demonstrators spent much of the night of 21–22 December on Bucharest's streets, especially around Piaţa Universităţii.

> To this day it is not known if the shots fired at the demonstrators throughout the revolution came from Ceauşescu loyalists or from supporters of the new regime, which – it has been suggested – needed martyrs to give itself credibility in the eyes of the people.

Ceauşescu and wife Elena fled by helicopter from the roof of the Central Committee building on the afternoon of the next day. Minutes later, demonstrators ransacked the building.

Inside, a new government was already being formed. Ion Iliescu, who until the early 1980s had been one of Ceauşescu's most loyal henchman, led a group calling itself the National Salvation Front (FSN). It officially declared itself the new government on 23 December. On Christmas Day, Ceauşescu and his wife were tried by a kangaroo court and shot in the town of Târgovişte.

The Shadow of Ion Iliescu

Despite promising initially that the FSN would be a purely transitional government, the organisation fielded candidates in elections of April 1990. Though these were allegedly free and fair, the FSN's absolute control of the media and all state apparatus meant that anything other than a resounding victory for the FSN and Iliescu – who ran for president – was never in question. Soon after, in early June 1990, appalled at the apparent replacement of one authoritarian regime with another, students and workers in Bucharest demonstrated against the new government, demanding that the FSN remove itself from politics, and that Iliescu step down. The demonstration was brutally put down by miners, brought in by Iliescu to do the job the Communist Securitate political police would have done in the old days. More than 100 demonstrators died in what became known as the *mineriada*.

Further demonstrations and a second *mineriada* in 1991 finally brought down the government, though Iliescu hung on, appointing a technocrat, Teodor Stolojan, to oversee the writing of a new constitution and to organise new elections in 1992. Though better-organised, the opposition was still soundly defeated. Iliescu remained president and his PDSR (the renamed FSN) formed a new government that became a byword for theft, corruption and economic stagnation.

After Iliescu

Iliescu was temporarily removed from power in 1996, only to be re-elected in 2000, having changed the constitution in order to be able to run for a third term. In 2004, unable to change the constitution yet again, he was finally forced to step down. His anointed successor, Adrian Nastase, was easily defeated by

A smile in Suceava, Moldavia

the populist Traian Basescu, the former mayor of Bucharest, who appointed a new government, relatively untainted by corruption and the 15 years of economic stagnation. With Romania set to join the EU in 2007 and Iliescu an old man unwanted even in his own party, the country does at last appear to have turned the corner towards a brighter future.

Historical Landmarks

513BC First recorded mention of the Geto-Dacians, the ancestors of the Romanians.

AD106–271 Dacia, comprising much of present-day Romania, is part of the Roman Empire.

c. 1300 The three Romanian principalities of Wallachia, Moldavia and Transylvania emerge from the Dark Ages as recognisable states.

1415 Wallachia becomes a vassal state of the Turks.

1541 Transylvania becomes part of the Ottoman Empire.

1687 Transylvania returned to Hungarian rule.

1877 Wallachia and Moldavia declare independence as Romania.

1919 Transylvania unified with Wallachia and Moldavia to form Greater Romania.

1941 Romania enters World War II on the side of the Axis powers.

1944 On 23 August Romania leaves the war, re-enters three days later on the side of the Allies.

1955 Romania a founding member of the Warsaw Pact and COMECON.

1979 Nicolae Ceauşescu is awarded a knighthood by Queen Elizabeth II of Britain.

1989 Ceauşescu is shot on Christmas Day after a popular revolution in which 1,033 die. Ion Iliescu, leader of the FSN, names himself the country's new leader.

1990 Elections confirm Iliescu as president.

1992 Iliescu re-elected as president for a four-year term. His renamed PDSR forms the government.

1996 Amid plummeting living standards Iliescu and the left-wing PDSR are defeated by a centre-right coalition. But the coalition is weak and unable to enact reform.

2000 Iliescu and the PDSR are returned to office.

2003 Romania is admitted to NATO.

2004 Former mayor of Bucharest Traian Basescu leads a centre-right coalition to power and becomes president.

2007 Romania due to join the EU.

WHERE TO GO

GETTING AROUND

Romania is a vast and diverse country whose poor communications make it difficult to explore in one trip. It is likely that you will return more than once, for if you want to see it all, you will have to. Train travel is slow, air travel expensive, and the country's road network so poor that driving is an option only for short distances.

Until Braşov – in so many ways the centre of Romania – gets itself an international airport, it is almost certain that you will arrive in Bucharest. This is both unfortunate and a boon. Unfortunate because you should be under no illusions about the capital's attractions: it is a dirty, noisy, often overwhelming city whose charms are not obvious. Yet it is perhaps unfair to dismiss this unique city out of hand. It is home to the country's best hotels, its best restaurants and its best shops.

BUCHAREST

Bucharest is a city of extremes and ironies: brand-new Audis speed along potholed streets, while old women in rags sell turnips on street corners. Summer temperatures often climb to over 40°C (105°F), though during the winter the city is covered in a blanket of snow for up to three months.

Piaţa Universităţii and Around

Bucharest lacks a real city centre, a focal point to which all roads lead. As such, a number of squares and piazzas have claims to be the centre, though that of **Piaţa Universităţii** is the strongest. It was here that the 1989 revolution gathered strength, and where pitched battles were fought from behind

The Palace of Parliament in Bucharest, viewed from Piaţa Unirii

King Michael the Brave rules over University Square

barricades. In the centre, **wooden crosses** and flowers commemorate those who died here on the night of 21–22 December 1989.

The square is overlooked by the enormous **Hotel Intercontinental**, built in 1970, which for almost 30 years was the tallest building in Romania. To its right is the **National Theatre** (Teatrul Naţional), built in the 1970s and redesigned in the late 1980s. Opposite the National Theatre is the main building of the **University of Bucharest**, from which the square gets its name. In front of the university, twin neoclassical buildings, built in an arc, were once the home of Bucharest's two richest families. Today one contains a bank, the other hosts a political party. Beside the twin buildings is the **Municipal Museum of Bucharest** (Muzeul Municipului Bucureşti; open Tues–Sun 10am–6pm; admission fee), housed in the former Şuţu Palace, where costumes, photos and paintings depict life in Bucharest in the 18th and 19th centuries.

North of Piaţa Universităţii is **Bulevardul General Magheru**, named after a legendary Romanian World War I general. Lined with expensive shops, art deco apartment blocks, hotels, theatres and casinos, it is the closest Bucharest has to a throbbing thoroughfare. It is also one of the busiest roads in Romania, and chock-full of traffic day and night.

At the far end of Bulevardul Magheru is **Piaţa Romană**, a huge junction of several important arteries. The one building of interest is the **Economics University** (ASE) on the northwestern side. Far more satisfactory is the **Piaţa Amzei** area to the southwest. This is the city's best-known market, where you will find the finest fruit and vegetables Romania has to offer.

Old Town

To the south and west of Piaţa Universităţii is the area known as Old Town, or more commonly **Lipscani**, all that remains of Old Bucharest. For centuries the area contained the city residences of the Romanian elite, before falling into disrepair during the communist era. Closed to all traffic except taxis, the area is undergoing extensive renovation. At its northern fringes, just behind Piaţa Universităţii is the **Russian Church** (Biserica Ruseasca), whose onion domes are a dead giveaway as to its roots. It was built between 1905 and 1909 with money from the Russian Patriarchate.

Deeper into the Lipscani area, the impressive **Romanian National Bank** (Banca Naţională a României) is a neoclassical gem dating from 1885. The banking hall inside is outstandingly preserved. A short walk from here along Str Lipscani is **Hanul cu Tei**, an alleyway – once a *han*, or inn – where you can pick up excellent-value arts, crafts and antiques in any of the small shops and workshops.

South of here, towards the river, Str Covaci will lead you past the Amsterdam Grand Café – one of the city's best –

A bookseller waits for trade outside the University

Inside the Palace of Parliament

to **Hanul lui Manuc**, a famous caravanserai where once traders and horsemen would drink in the inn above, their horses in the stables below. Many of the original features remain, including the splendid entrance and courtyard, now a rather ordinary Romanian restaurant. The Hanul is popular for weddings, and if you come here on any Saturday evening in the summer you are likely to see a Romanian wedding party in full flow. Opposite is the sublime **Old Court Church** (Biserica Curtea Veche). It is the oldest church in Bucharest (1559), and the astonishing frescos inside are original. In front are the ruins of the **Old Court** (Curtea Veche) itself, where Vlad Țepeș established his capital in the 15th century.

The Civic Centre

Few experiments in urban planning have gone so dreadfully wrong as that which saw most of Old Bucharest destroyed and rebuilt to the grandiose vision of a megalomaniac in the

1980s. Piaţa Unirii, the heart of what became known as the **Civic Centre**, had for centuries been the soul of Bucharest. When the charming old square and more than 20,000 houses and 70 churches around it were destroyed, to be replaced with hastily built apartment blocks and endless expanses of concrete, Bucharest lost any trace of that soul.

There can be no building in the world as soulless as the **Palace of Parliament** (Palatul Parlamentului; guided tours only, daily 10am–4pm; admission fee), which dominates the Civic Centre and most of Bucharest. It was built between 1984 and 1990 on one of the city's few hills, and on the site of the Mihai Vodă Monastery (which was destroyed to make way for the palace; even the hill was levelled slightly).

The palace was built using only materials from Romania, and the guided tour of this masterpiece of neoclassical post-modern kitsch is well worthwhile. From the **balcony** you will get the defining view of Communist-era Bucharest, along Bulevardul Unirii and out towards the rest of the Civic Centre, Piaţa Unirii and Piaţa Alba Iulia. The building today houses Romania's parliament, as well as the **Museum of Contemporary Art** (Muzeul Naţional de Artă Contempor-ana; open Tues–Sun 10am–6pm; admission fee).

About 1km (half a mile) back towards the city centre, along Bulevardul Unirii, is **Piaţa Unirii**, one of the world's

Quake!

Central and Southern Romania is one of Europe's liveliest earthquake zones. Fortunately, the recent trend has been towards regular, medium-strength tremors – which can be terrifying if you are living or staying on an upper floor, but do no real damage – rather than occasional major quakes. The last serious earthquake hit Bucharest in 1977, causing vast damage and killing more than 1,500 people.

largest public squares. Starting from the southwestern corner of the square is a road leading uphill to the **Patriarchal Cathedral and Monastery** (Catedrala Patriarchala), known colloquially by locals as Mitropoliei after the small hill on which it stands. The cathedral, built between 1654 and 1658, was designed to resemble the Curtea de Argeş in Piteşti *(see page 37)*, but little of the original structure remains. The splendid icons all date from 1923, except that depicting **Constantine and Elena**, an original from 1665. The complex of buildings behind the cathedral makes up the Patriarchal Palace, the official residence of Teoctist, the Patriarch of the Romanian Orthodox Church. It is also a working monastery, and strictly off-limits to visitors.

Cotroceni to Cismigiu

Since 1990, Romania's president has lived in the splendid **Cotroceni Palace and Museum** (guided tours only, Tues–Sun 10am–5pm; admission fee; tel: 021-430 61 71). Here in Cotroceni, the city's leafiest suburb (and the one most untouched by Communist-era construction), the palace was built by King Ferdinand and his English wife Marie, whose hand is evident everywhere.

Beside the palace is the city's **Botanical Garden** (Grădina Botanică; garden open daily 8am–5pm, glasshouses open Tues, Thur, Sat, Sun 9am–1pm; admission fee). The garden, laid out in 1884, is home to a wide variety of flora and fauna, and includes some impressive landscapes.

Making your way back into town along the river you will come to **Piaţa Eroilor**, one of the best-kept squares in the city, with small but splendid lawns and a children's play area. On the southern side are two churches of note, **Biserica Sf Elefterie Nou** and **Biserica Sf Elefterie Vechi** (New and Old Churches of St Elefterus). The newer church, built in 1922, is the very Russian-looking rust-and-green-striped

Orthodox priests outside the Patriarchal Cathedral and Monastery

affair which towers over the square. The older church, built in 1864 and now in the middle of a roundabout, is the more charming, with many original frescos surviving.

On the square's northern side (across the river Dâmboviţa), fronted by a small garden and a statue of George Enescu, is the **Romanian National Opera** (Opera Naţională Română). It was built in 1950–2 and betrays a rather unimaginative, neoclassical design. The Opera hosts first-class performances most evenings, and tickets are cheap. The box office in the foyer is open daily from 10am–noon.

A short, rewarding walk west along **Bulevardul Mihai Kogălniceanu** (notable for its art-nouveau 1920s apartment blocks, many of which are at risk of falling during Bucharest's next earthquake) takes you past the University of Bucharest's Law Faculty, past Piaţa Mihai Kogălniceanu (a statue of Kogălniceanu, a 19th-century revolutionary, stands in the middle of the square), and brings you to one of the many entrances of **Cismigiu Park** (Grădina Cişmigiu). Bucharest's most central park was laid out from 1845–60 by the Austrian Carl Meyer, and is busy at all times of day, every day of the year.

Calea Victoriei

Bucharest's most celebrated street is **Calea Victoriei**, which meanders its way from Piaţa Victoriei in the north, down through the city centre to the river Dâmboviţa. It's worth walking the entire length, from south to north, beginning at the Dâmboviţa, and stopping first at the **National History Museum** (Muzeul Naţional de Istorie; open Wed–Sun 10am–5pm; admission fee). The museum is not great, as many of the pre-1989 exhibits dedicated to the Communist regime have been removed, only for the void to remain empty. The best sections are those in the basement relating to the Roman period, including a cast of Trajan's Column in Rome.

Grand façades on Calea Victoriei

Directly opposite the museum is the **CEC Building** (Casa de Economii si Consemnaţiuni), whose fabulous façade is one of the city's best. It is less impressive inside. Across Bulevardul Regina Elisabeta, the Military Club (Cercul Militar, 1912) is on the left, with the historic Casa Capşa hotel and restaurant on the other side of the road.

Following the curve of the road, you will soon arrive at **Piaţa Revoluţiei**, the city's most historic square. It was here that the Communist regime came to an end in December 1989, when Nicolae Ceauşescu fled from the roof of the Central Committee Building (now the Romanian Senate, Senatul Roman) as demonstrators broke in. The

> The Royal Palace was built in 1812 by the wealthy landowner Dinicu Golescu, but became state property in 1859 when his sons squandered their inheritance. It was the home of Romania's royal family until 1947, when its last resident, King Mihai, fled into exile.

balcony from which the dictator made his final address is pointed out – literally – by a small memorial to the revolution. A much larger monument now towers rather awkwardly above the square. Locals refer to it as 'the olive on a tooth-pick'. Bullet-holes visible in the walls of the Humanitas book-shop opposite are a more fitting reminder of those mad December days.

The church in front of the bookshop is the recently reno-vated **Creţulescu Church** (Biserica Creţulescu; 1720–2). To the left of the church is the enormous former **Royal Palace**, today the **National Art Museum** (Muzeul Naţional de Artă; open Wed–Sun, 11am–7pm May–Sep, 10am–6pm Oct–Apr; admission fee). The country's foremost art gallery, it houses works by all of Romania's greatest painters, including Nico-lae Grigorescu, Theodor Aman and Gheorghe Tatarescu. It also has a vast collection of Old European Masters.

Piaţa Revoluţiei's northern side is dominated by the Athe-nee Palace Hilton hotel. Opposite the Hilton is the remark-able **Ateneul Roman** (Roman Atheneum), a stunning late 19th-century neoclassical concert hall, today the home of the Romanian Philharmonic George Enescu. You can only see inside if attending a concert, held most evenings.

Piața Victoriei to Herăstrău

Calea Victoriei emerges at Piața Victoriei, another vast square of tower blocks, concrete and traffic. Its two saving graces are the sleek lines of the **Victoria Palace** (Palatul din Piața Victoriei, 1937), the home of Romania's government, and the **Peasant Museum** (Muzeul Țăranului; open Tues–Sun 10am–6pm; admission fee), just north of the square. This is the city's best museum, full of well-presented exhibits that tell the story of the Romanian peasant. In the basement is a small but superb exhibition dedicated to **Communist iconography**, the one place in Romania you will see a portrait of Nicolae Ceaușescu. The museum also houses one of the best souvenir shops in the country.

> Violinist and composer George Enescu (1881–1955) was a giant of modern music, although the majority of his works, including the sublime *Romanian Rhapsody*, remain little-known outside Romania. Calea Victoriei 141, Enescu's former home, is today a museum (open Tues–Sun 10am–5pm; admission fee)

A long but rewarding walk the length of Șos. Kiseleff, full of fine villas, past the **Arc de Triumf**, will bring you to the **Village Museum** (Muzeul Satului; open Mon 10am–5pm, Tues–Sun 9am–7pm; admission fee), a collection of original houses, wooden churches and other buildings from the Romanian countryside, brought to Bucharest by Royal Decree in 1936. The Village Museum is actually part of **Herăstrău Park**, the city's largest open space. It has a lake in the middle, surrounded by a number of good terraces, a children's play area and a small, rather outdated funfair. You can also take short pleasure cruises around the lake.

At the head of Șos Kiseleff is the monstrous **Casa Scân-teii**, built in the early 1950s and modelled on the Palace of city centre. From the 13th to the 17th centuries Romanians were forbidden from owning property within the city walls, so they settled outside in what is today the Schei district. For centuries Braşov was one of the most important towns on the Vienna–Constantinople route, and its trade links made it wealthy.

Modern Braşov is the most visited city in Romania, not least during the Carpathian Stag Song Festival, held during July or September. No visit to the country is complete without spending a couple of days here.

Most visitors begin their time in Braşov with the clas-

View of Braşov from Mt Tampa

sic walk along **Bulevardul Republicii**, a cobbled, pedestrianised street that leads to Piaţa Sfatului, the heart of the Old Town. But before you do, duck into the excellent **Ethnography Museum** (Muzeul de Etnografie; open Wed–Sat 10am–5pm; admission fee) on Bulevardul Eroilor, opposite the city's largest park, Parcul Central, and the small but charming **Art Museum** (Muzeul de Artă; open Tues–Sun 10am–6pm; admission fee) next to it. The Art Museum has a particularly good selection of paintings by 19th-century Impressionist Nicolae Grigorescu, currently the most sought-after Romanian painter.

Bulevardul Republicii is a surprisingly wide street, most of whose buildings lack care and attention, but whose charms are overwhelming. During the summer, street cafés and terraces

The 15th-century Council Hall in the middle of Piaţa Sfatului

fill up early and empty very late, while in winter snow crunches under the feet of après-skiers looking for the right hostelry to dine or drink in. The choice is endless, with bars, cafés, pubs and restaurants all the way up to, and around, **Piaţa Sfatului**.

The large square, which the Saxons called Marktplatz, is dominated by the old **Casa Sfatului** (Council Hall) in the middle. Built in 1420 – though the tower, once used as a lookout post for approaching Ottomans, is slightly older – it today houses the rather dull **Braşov History Museum** (Muzeul de Istorie a Braşovului; open Tues–Sun 10am–6pm). Surrounding the square on all sides are classic Saxon houses, famed for their high upper levels, one of which is now put to use as a shopping mall. On the southern side of the square is the **Romanian Orthodox Cathedral** (Catedrala Ortodoxǎ Româna), a late-19th-century copy of a Byzantine church.

South of Piaţa Sfatului is the single most impressive sight in Braşov, the **Black Church** (Biserica Neagra; open Mon–

Sat 10am–3.30pm; admission fee). Built between 1385 and 1477, and first called the Marienkirche, it was blackened during a fire in 1689 that destroyed much of the city. It has been known as the Black Church ever since. It is the tallest European church east of Vienna.

Leading back to Parcul Central is **Str Mureşenilor**, a commercial street full of shops (including two or three good ski-equipment stores) and a number of bars and restaurants. West of here is Str Dupa Ziduri (Street Behind the Wall), along which are crumbling remnants of Braşov's **old city wall**, and three of the city's original towers, the White Tower, Black Tower and Blacksmiths' Bastion. Confusingly, the Black Tower is the white one. The wall disappears for a short time, then reappears at the sublime **Catherine's Gate**, built in 1559 and once the city's main entrance. A short walk from here is the equally well-preserved **Weavers' Bastion** (Bastionul Tesatorilor; open Tues–Sun 10am–5.30pm; admission fee). The bastion is the best-preserved portion of the city's fortifications, and contains an impressive scale model of Braşov c. 1600.

The best way to approach the **Schei** district is the way Romanians did for centuries: through Catherine's Gate. A short walk along the winding Str Poarta Schei, past Braşov's **Synagogue** (open Mon–Fri 10am–1pm), will bring you to the district's centre, **Piaţa Unirii**. On the left is the beautiful **St Nicholas' Church** (Biserica Sf Nicolae), originally built in 1521 in Byzantine style, and expanded in the 18th century, when the sleek

Imposing Catherine's Gate was once Braşov's main entrance

tower and four turrets were added, making it far more Saxon in appearance. In the grounds is the grave of Nicolae Titulescu, the statesman, diplomat and one-time leader of the League of Nations. He died in exile in Switzerland in 1941, was buried in Cannes, and his remains were only brought here in 1990. Next to the church is the outstanding **First Romanian School Museum** (Prima Biserică Românească; open Tues–Sun 10am–6pm; admission fee), which was, as the name suggests, the first school anywhere to teach in the Romanian language (it opened in 1495).

From here, it is worth setting off further into Schei, admiring the old houses, so closely packed, and walking as far as **Solomon's Rocks** (Pietrele lui Solomon), two natural outcrops of rock which locals claim were an act of God. This bizarre but gorgeous setting is also the location for the *Juni* dances, which take place on the first Sunday in May. The young men of Schei (the *Juni*) assemble in Piața Unirii and march here to dance, to celebrate the coming of spring.

Poiana Brașov

The easiest way to the ski resort of **Poiana Brașov** is along the modern 12-km (7-mile) route that begins next to the Astra Cinema in central Brașov. Buses from here make the trip in around 40 minutes, cars significantly less, though on weekend afternoons in the ski season the queues to get into the resort can snake halfway down to Brașov.

Poiana has long been a retreat for the wealthy, but it only became a ski resort in the 1950s, when the first cable-car was built. The resort was much developed in the 1960s, with a number of large hotels being built for Western package tourists. There are now two cable-cars, a gondola lift and three drag lifts. Queues at the weekend are obscene, though during the week you can often feel like the only skier in the resort. There are around 15km (9 miles) of piste, and a good skier will ski the entire resort in a morning. Snow is usually guaranteed from December to mid-March, and ski equipment can be hired from any number of places. In winter you can enjoy long horse-drawn **sleigh rides** through the forest.

Poiana remains busy during the summer, and mountain biking is increasingly popular. However, the main summer activity is walking. Romanians like to take the cable-car up the mountain and take a leisurely walk down. There are plenty of marked routes.

Wooden church in Poiana Braşov

The Prahova Valley

The ski resort of **Predeal** is the highest town in Romania, set at the top of the pass that links Transylvania with Wallachia, at an altitude of 1,100m (3,600ft). Though skiing is limited to just 10km (6 miles) of piste, the resort did recently install a new chair-lift, which is one of the fastest in the country. The nursery slopes are particularly suited to children, and there are any number of ski schools and independent ski instructors around to teach beginners. Besides skiing there is little to do in Predeal, though during the summer the chairlift remains open to whisk walkers up to the top of the mountain. There are hiking routes from here over to Azuga.

At the end of a winding mountain road that begins at the Orizont Hotel is the tiny resort of **Trei Brazi**. There is a large but

The view from Cota 1400, Sinaia

somewhat run-down hotel here, which has a good terrace and restaurant. There are great walks into the woods from here, and you can hire quad-bikes, mountain bikes and, in winter, snowmobiles.

Azuga is another of Romania's one-chair-lift ski resorts, 5km (3 miles) from Predeal. It is a nice enough town, but the aesthetics are somewhat ruined by large factories at the town's entrance. Azuga is home to one of Romania's best breweries, where the light, crisp Azuga beer is made, and there is also the fabulous **Rhein-Azuga Wine Cellar** (open daily 10am–4pm except in winter), where you can learn about the process of making the superb Rhein Extra Champenoise sparkling wine.

Past Azuga, heading south, the Bucegi Mountains begin to loom almost menacingly on the horizon. Becoming very abrupt, they peak at the next resort along the road, **Buşteni**, long the Romanian capital of hiking and walking. A cable-car from close to the Silva Hotel takes walkers up to over 2,000m (6,560ft), from where a number of walks – many quite challenging – fan out in all directions, including one that takes walkers as far as Bran. More recently a modern chair-lift has been installed at Buşteni to serve Romania's newest ski slope, **Kalinderu**. The chair-lift is found 2km (1 mile) from the centre of Buşteni, and is well signposted.

Sinaia

Set at a cooling 800m (2,620ft), and originally the retreat of kings and hermit monks, **Sinaia** (which takes its name from the 17th-century Sinaia Monastery, in turn named after Mount Sinai) is today a rather overgrown sprawl of a place, half industrial town and half mountain resort. Yet it has more charm than all of Romania's other mountain resorts put together. The skiing here, high up at 2,000m (6,560ft), accessed by the two-stage cable-car behind the Montana Hotel, is the best and most challenging in the country, and there is often enough snow for skiing as late as May. When the snow is particularly good you can ski the 12km (7 miles) down to Sinaia itself.

A short walk through the resort's main park, situated at the end of its main street, Bulevardul Carol I, leads to the stunning **Sinaia Monastery** (Mănăstirea Sinaia; open Wed–Sun, 10am–6pm; admission fee), founded by Mihai

Brown Bears

Romania contains Europe's largest population of bears – as many as 6,400 of them, approximately half of all the brown bears in Europe. In 1989 there were as many as 8,000. They live at an altitude of around 1,000m (3,000ft) throughout the full arc of the Carpathian mountain range. Small numbers of bears are hunted each year, though these are usually problem animals identified by the authorities as dangerous to the overall well-being of a group, and the high charges paid by hunters for the privilege of shooting them (as much as €7,000 each bear) helps fund conservation programmes, which in turn have stabilised the bear population. Around 300 are shot each year. Contact with people is more and more common, as many bears have become semi-domesticated (especially around Braşov), scavenging in bins for food. Bears are usually scared of humans, but you should never approach one, as attacks on people, while rare, are not unknown.

Peleş Castle, built for Romania's German king, Carol I

Cantacuzino in 1682 after a pilgrimage to the Holy Land. There are two churches: Biserica Veche (Old Church), dating from 1695, and Biserica Mare (Great Church), built in 1846. The large mausoleum in the forecourt of the monastery houses the body of Tache Ionescu, who was a Romanian *fin-de-siècle* diplomat.

Peleş Castle (Castelul Peleş) was built to order between 1874 and 1883 for Romania's first modern king, Carol I, who used it as his summer residence. It is an extraordinary Germanic, neo-Renaissance construction designed by the Viennese architect Wilhelm Doderer. Tours of the castle (open Wed–Sun 9am–3pm; admission fee) are available in any number of languages. The smaller **Pelişor** complex in the grounds (open Wed–Sun 9am–3pm; admission included in ticket for main castle) was the preferred mountain retreat of Queen Marie, the English wife of Carol's successor, King Ferdinand.

Day Trips from Braşov

The **Medieval Citadel** at **Râşnov** (Cetatea Râşnovului; open 10am–5pm; admission fee), about 15km (9 miles) west of Braşov, is one of the best-preserved in the whole of Romania. It stands imposingly at the top of a steep hill, overlooking the vast plain below. The citadel was first built by the Teutonic Knights in the 12th century, and once housed much of the population of the village below. The citadel was supplied with water by a well – which survives to this day – dug over 16 years by two Turkish prisoners in exchange for their freedom. The road up to the citadel from Râşnov is steep, and a tough walk. It is best to drive; the route is well signposted. The village of Râşnov itself is served by train from Braşov, but is not particularly interesting.

Just 12km (7 miles) further is the even more spectacular **Bran Castle** (Castelul Bran; open Tues–Sun 9am–5pm; admission fee; guided tours). Over the past century it has become known as Dracula's Castle, though the link between Vlad Ţepeş and the castle is weak at best, and probably non-existent (*see box, page 52*). What is certain is that the castle was built around 1360, and that in 1441 Vlad Ţepeş defeated the Turks near here, and may well have used the castle as a residence for a while afterwards. Either way, it certainly looks as though it should be Dracula's Castle, and it's easy to see why it inspired Bram Stoker (who saw it only in pictures). At the foot of the castle there is a large, somewhat touristy market, but you can pick up great souvenirs if you are prepared to haggle a little.

Young visitors to Bran Castle

After years of negotiation and bitter legal battles, in 2006 the Romanian state returned Bran Castle to its rightful owner: New York architect Dominic von Hapsburg, the great-grandson of King Ferdinand. As part of the settlement, von Hapsburg must keep the castle open as a museum at least until 2009.

Bran and neighbouring **Moeciu** are great bases to explore the surrounding mountains by car. They are also the centre of Romania's growing agro-tourism sector, and a number of pensions and guesthouses can be found at very reasonable prices, offering full board: a great way to sample genuine Transylvanian cuisine. Try the agro-tourism websites Cazari <www.cazari.ro> or Antrec <www.antrec.ro>.

The gateway to the superb **Făgăraş Mountains** is the rather dull industrial town of Făgăraş, whose one point of interest, its once superb 15th-century castle, is a wilfully neglected pile crying out for renovation. Far more worthy of your time is the stunning monastery at **Sâmbata de Sus**, about 25km (15 miles) west of Făgăraş. The monastery (open Mon–Sat 10am–5pm, Sun 1–5pm; admission fee) was founded by the Wallachian prince Constantin Brâncoveanu, and completed in 1698. Much of what we see today is the result of extensive renovation in the 1930s, but many of the exhibits in the

In the Făgăraş Mountains

monastery's **Glass Icon Museum** (Muzeul de Icoane pe Sticlă) are original. A workshop in the grounds still produces glass icons.

If you are looking to do some serious hiking in the Făgăraş range, Sâmbata is a good base. One of the shortest routes up to **Moldoveanu** (Romania's highest peak) begins here.

Sibiu

Always considered the most German of Romanian cities, **Sibiu** is not without reason the most civilised place in the country. It has a superb city centre, based on three large *piaţas*, Mare, Mică and Huet, a well-preserved Old Town,

and a thriving commercial heart along the pedestrianised Str Nicolae Bălcescu. Even the newer parts, around Piața Unirii, are less dreary than in most Romanian cities.

Sibiu, always a Saxon town, was known as Hermannstadt during the years when the Habsburgs ruled this region (as it is today to the few Germans who still live here), and served as the capital of Habsburg Transylvania. It therefore has an imperial feel unlike any other city in the country.

Nowhere is that imperial heritage more obvious than in the large central square, **Piața Mare**, with its **Council Tower** (Turnul Sfatului; open Tues–Sat 10am–5pm; admission fee), built in 1588, overlooking the square and much of the city. From the top you can see as far as the Făgăraș Mountains in the distance.

Sibiu Old Town

Situated just to the right of the tower is the city's **Roman Catholic Cathedral** (Catedrala Romano-Catolică), a rather plain construction completed in 1733. On the western side of the square is the far more interesting **Brukenthal Museum** (Muzeul Brukenthal; open Tues–Sun 9am–5pm summer, 10am–4pm winter; admission fee), a wonderful collection of art housed in the former residence of the Habsburg governor of Transylvania, Samuel Brukenthal. To the left of the museum is the former City Hall, allegedly the oldest Gothic building in Romania, and today the **Sibiu History Museum** (Muzeul de Istorie a Municipului Sibiu; open Tues–Sun 9am–5pm; admission fee). The museum tells the story of the city well, and

> **Linking Piaţa Huet to Piaţa Mica is the Bridge of Lies (Podul Minciunilor), on which it is said anyone who tells a lie will cause the bridge to collapse.**

began life when Brukenthal handed over a number of his own possessions in the late 18th century. You will see further evidence of Brukenthal's benevolence all over the city.

A number of other sights cluster around the smaller squares of Piaţa Mică and Piaţa Huet. Worth investigating are the vast Gothic **Evangelical Cathedral** on Piaţa Huet, which contains Romania's largest pipe organ and the tomb of Prince Mihnea cel Rău (Mihnea the Bad), the son of Vlad Ţepeş. There are two museums on Piaţa Mică: the **Pharmarceutical Museum** (open Tues–Sun 10am–4pm; admission fee) and the **Franz Binder Museum of Ethnology** (Tues–Sun 10am–5pm; admission fee). Neither is really worth your time. Instead, head along the road that leads under the Bridge of Lies into the **Old Town**, and take a walk around the narrow streets full of old Saxon houses, with their distinctive red roof tiles and high courtyard gates.

Sibiu's commercial thoroughfare, Str Nicolae Bălcescu, is a street of low-rise shops and restaurants, terraces and old-fashioned cinemas. On summer evenings the promenade along here is positively Mediterranean, though the architecture is strictly Saxon. Some of the buildings have seen better days, but they nevertheless retain real charm. Just behind Str Nicolae Bălcescu, on Str Mitropoliei, is the city's **Orthodox Cathedral** (Catedrala Ortodoxă Sf Treime), which dates from 1906. The ornate exterior is complemented by a superb wooden interior, centred on a huge dome and a golden altar. The impressive altar frescos were added in the 1950s.

Str Nicolae Bălcescu tips out into the vast but well-kept and green Piaţa Unirii, faced on its northern side by the monolithic Hotel Bulevard. East of the square, behind Str Cetatii is a well-preserved section of Sibiu's **old city walls**. The large building on the west of the square is the City Hall (Primarie).

Don't miss a trip to the **Astra Museum of Folk Civilisation** (Muzeul Civilizatiei Populare Traditionale Astra; open mid-Apr–Oct Tues–Sun 10am–6pm; admission fee), which is set over 80 hectares (200 acres) around a huge lake south of Sibiu. It contains more than 340 original houses, churches, workshops and windmills from all over Transylvania, designed to show off the skills of the Romanian peasant. In high summer, folklore shows are put on here.

Sighişoara

Better known internationally than Sibiu, and widely viewed as Romania's number-one attraction, the medieval town of **Sighişoara** can actually be a bit of a let-down. Certainly,

Creation of a Vampire

The myth of Dracula is purely a figment of Bram Stoker's imagination. The author never visited Romania, but was obsessed with the stories of Vlad Dracul and his son Vlad Ţepeş, who brutally put down a number of Turkish invasions, usually impaling any prisoners on spikes. *Dracul* is one of many Romanian words for the devil, and it is that fact which allegedly persuaded Stoker that the name was perfect for the villain of his 1897 novel. Most Romanians find the Dracula myth tiresome, though they never hestitate to cash in on the connection between Transylvania and the legend. There have so far been three attempts to build a Dracula theme park.

the medieval **city walls** are among the best-preserved in Europe, with nine of the 12 original towers still standing, but besides walking around the old city there is precious little to do. The one exception is in July, when the three-day Sighişoara Medieval Arts Festival welcomes tens of thousands of students who party through the night, sleeping rough on the medieval city's streets.

Modern Sighişoara is as grim as any other modern town in Romania, so you should head straight for the **Citadel**, accessed via a relatively steep path that leads up from Piaţa Hermann Oberth.

The Old Town and Clock Tower

You enter the citadel through the immense **Clock Tower** (Turnul cu Ceas; open Mon–Sat 10am–5pm, Sun 10am–3.30pm; admission fee), once the main entrance to the walled city. It stands 64m (210ft) tall, and you can climb to the top. At the foot of the tower is a Torture Museum and a display of medieval arms, both free using the Clock Tower entrance ticket. Inside the citadel is the 15th-century **Monastery Church** (Biserica Mănăstirii), famous for its fine baroque altarpiece from 1680. Opposite is **Dracula's House** (Casa Vlad Dracul), where Vlad Ţepeş was allegedly born in 1414. Today it is a rather good Transylvanian restaurant, with awful service.

Heading left from here you will come to the **Covered Stairway** (Pasajul Scarilor), an extraordinary walkway that leads up to the **Church of the Hill** (Biserica din Deal), a 15th-century structure whose exquisite frescos and wood carvings were fully restored in 1995–6. Next to the church is the German Cemetery, and beside that the superb **Gold-smiths' Tower** (Turnul Aurarilor), the best-preserved of Sighişoara's original defence positions.

Cluj-Napoca

The most cosmopolitan city in the country, **Cluj-Napoca** rivals Sibiu, Timişoara and Braşov as being the best place in Romania in which to live. It also has excellent restaurants, bars and clubs, and its large student population provides a raucous nightlife. The city's name was originally just Cluj: Napoca was added in 1974 to highlight the town's links to Roman Napoca, which stood close to the modern city.

Dominating Cluj-Napoca's central square, Piaţa Unirii, is the enormous St Michael's **Roman Catholic Church** (Biserica Romano-Catolică Sf Mihai), one of the finest Gothic buildings in Romania. In front of the church is a statue of Matei Corvin on horseback. The splendid **National Art Museum** (Muzeul Naţional de Artă; open Wed–Sun 10am–5pm; admission fee) stands behind and to the left of the church. Housed in a baroque mansion built in the 1760s for the governor of Transylvania, the museum is a treasure trove of exquisite glass icons, silverware and furniture.

A news kiosk in Cluj-Napoca

On the other side of the Catholic church, a short walk along Str Memorandului, is the equally impressive

A bar on Piaţa Unirii in Cluj-Napoca

Ethnographic Museum (Muzeul Etnografic; open Tues–Sun 9am–5pm; admission fee; guided tours). This was fully renovated in 2005 and is now one of Romania's best museums. A superb collection of clearly labelled artefacts, costumes, diagrams and maps delightfully tells the story of the Transylvanian peasant through the ages. An open-air section of the museum, with windmills, sawmills, workshops and farmhouses, is situated in a small park on Str Taietura Turcului, 5km (3 miles) north of the city centre (open May–Nov Tues–Sun 10am–4pm; admission fee). Bus No. 22 will get you there.

The area around **Piaţa Muzeului** is the oldest part of Cluj-Napoca, mercifully spared by the Communist bulldozers. The houses here are typical of Transylvania, many with internal courtyards and balustraded balconies. Piaţa Muzeului itself is dominated by the museum which gives it its name, the **National History Museum of Transylvania** (Muzeul Naţional

A roadside crafts shop outside Cluj-Napoca

de Istorie al Transylvaniei; open Tues–Sun 10am–4pm; admission fee; guided tours). There are a huge number of exhibits, all of them presented in context and comprehensively detailing Transylvania's disputed past. Opposite the museum is the Fransciscan Church, reputedly the city's oldest, dating from 1486 and founded by Matei Corvin.

The **Romanian Orthodox Cathedral** (Catedrala Ortodoxă), in Piața Avram Iancu a short walk east from Piața Unirii, is a modern building, dating from the 1920s, and is rather plain. Its size, rather than its form or decoration, was meant to impress and inspire the faithful. Meanwhile, the **Botanical Gardens** (Grădina Botanică; open Tues–Sun 9am–8pm; greenhouses open 10am–4pm; admission fee), south of the city centre on Str Gheorghe Bilascu, are splendid. They spread over 15 hectares (37 acres) and contain more than 600 different varieties of flowers. There is a super Japanese Garden, and the greenhouses are endlessly fascinating.

South of Cluj-Napoca

An hour or so's drive south of Cluj-Napoca, through some stunning scenery at the foothills of the Apuseni Mountains, is the historic city of **Alba Iulia**. It was here on 1 December 1918 that Transylvania's Romanians declared themselves independent of Hungary (official recognition came a year later). The city's one sight of note is the enormous **Citadel** that dominates the surrounding area. A fortress has stood here since the 13th century, though most of what we see today is from the 18th, when much of the citadel was rebuilt. Unification Hall, in which independence was proclaimed, is in the very centre of the citadel.

Southwest of Alba Iulia is **Deva**, another town with a citadel that has seen better days, and it is not really worth stopping here. Far more impressive than Deva is the monstrous **Corvin Castle** at **Hunedoara** to the south. The castle (Castelul Corvin; open Tues–Sun 9am–5pm; admission fee) was built in the 14th century on the site of an old Roman fort, and was the power base of Iancu of Hundedoara, who slowly spread his sphere of influence and eventually installed himself as regent of Hungary. It is easy to see why the castle evoked power: its size is overwhelming and its location impenetrable.

Constantin Brâncusi

No Romanian artist has captured the world's attention as much as sculptor Constantin Brâncusi (1867–1957). Romanians quip that he is so well known that most art lovers assume he was a Frenchman. He certainly lived his professional life in Paris, but his work reflects a Balkan influence. In his later years, Brâncusi produced a series of immense public artworks, including the *Infinite Column*, which are today on display in the western city of Târgu Jiu, his birthplace.

BANAT AND MARAMUREŞ

A large minority of the population in the western region is Hungarian, which gives it a very European air. After centuries as part of the Hungarian and Habsburg Empire, most of the region has only been part of Romania since 1918. Old habits die hard, and visitors arriving from Bucharest or the south can be forgiven for thinking they have arrived in a different country. Yet the north of the region, known as the Maramureş, could well lay claim to being to the most traditional area of Romania. In a country of contrasts, few are as clear as those in Romania's west and northwest.

Timişoara

A city of parks and churches, **Timişoara** is perhaps the most Western-looking city in Romania. It is the third-largest city in the country (population 400,000), and the most important challenger to the commercial supremacy of the capital. Timişoara was founded by Hungarians in the 13th century, and found fame after Charles Robert of Anjou built a palace here shortly before naming himself Hungarian king (Károly Róbert) in 1316, when he at once made Timişoara Hungary's capital. After a century and a half of Ottoman rule (1552–1716) the city became part of the Habsburg Empire, until it was absorbed into Romania under the terms of the Treaty of Versailles.

Timişoara played a major role in the 1989 revolution when László Tökés, the priest of the Hungarian Reformed Church, was due to be sent to a small parish outside of the city in punishment for preaching anti-regime sermons. To prevent the eviction, parishioners surrounded the church in such numbers that the protest soon developed into a nationwide revolution.

Timişoara is a major university town, and also one of Romania's leading nightlife venues. In summer, crowds assemble on the many terraces of Piaţa Victoriei before moving on to the bars, pubs and clubs of Piaţa Unirii and the Old Town when darkness falls. The promenade along Str Alba Iulia from one part of the town to the other is positively Mediterranean.

The modern centre of Timişoara is the large, rectangular **Piaţa Victoriei**, dominated at one end by the green-and-gold domes of the cathedral, and at the other by the Opera House. The neo-Byzantine **Orthodox Cathedral** (open daily 6am– 8pm; free) was built between 1936–46, and at 83m (272ft) the main dome is one of the largest in the country. Inside, the four columns of the central dome are decorated with superb **frescos** of the apostles by local master Anastasie Demian.

Immediately in front of the cathedral is the **Monument to the Revolutionaries of 1989** (Eroilor Revoluţiei din 1989), a striking modernist memorial in bright aluminium. The memorial sits in a fine, well-kept garden, overlooked by rather bleak apartment blocks on one side and rather more

Piaţa Victoriei and the Orthodox Cathedral in Timişoara

interesting Habsburg-era buildings on the other. Street cafés and lively terraces line both sides of the square. At the far end, directly opposite the cathedral, is the starkly modernist **State Opera House and National Theatre**.

Opposite the Opera, and to the right of Piaţa Revolutiei, is the **Hunyadi Palace** (Palatul Hunyadi), built in the 14th century and the home of Robert of Anjou when Temesvar was the capital of Hungary. Inside the palace, the **Banat Museum** (Muzeul Banatului; open Tues–Sun 10am–4.30pm; admission fee) displays a reasonably interesting collection of artefacts and informative displays from the Geto-Dacian, Roman, medieval and 19th-century eras, but – given Timişoara's role in the revolution – is disappointingly weak on modern history. In front of the palace entrance two street lamps mark the spot where, in 1884, Timişoara became the first city in Europe to have electric street lights.

Opposite the palace, the pedestrianised Str Alba Iulia, awash with tsrendy cafés and shops, leads to **Piaţa Libertăţii**. To the north is the Old Town, to the west is the modern commercial district, including the Bega Shopping Centre on Str Proclomaţia de la Timişoara, next to the monolithic

The Banat Museum

Continental Hotel. South of the Orthodox Cathedral, bordering the river, are a number of large parks, many with restaurants and terraces, which fill up early during the summer.

Your first stop in the **Old Town** should be the enormous **Synagogue** on Str Mărăşeşti. The synagogue went up in 1865, just a year after Jews had been given

Piața Unirii is the heart of Timișoara's Old Town

land rights by Emperor Franz Joseph. It is closed for renovation until at least 2008. In fact, much of the Old Town is currently being renovated, though the overall aesthetic of the area, with its two-storey Hungarian-style houses, is well preserved.

A short walk north is **Piața Unirii**, the centrepiece of the Old Town. The first sight you will see is the very yellow **Serbian Orthodox Church**, built 1744–8. The interior is superb, with fine frescos added in the 19th century by Constantin Daniel. On the other side of the square stands the equally historic **Roman Catholic Cathedral**, completed in 1736. The interior is simple, brightened only by a spectacular golden altarpiece. In the centre of the square is the **Holy Trinity Monument** (Sf Treime), erected in 1740 (originally in Piața Transylvania) to give thanks for the passing of the bubonic plague which ravaged Timișoara in 1738–9. Dominating the southern side of the square is Timișoara's **Old Town Hall** (Primarie Veche), built on the site of a former Turkish bath between 1731 and 1734.

The rest of the Old Town's streets, laid out in a simple grid system during an urban-renewal programme in the 1890s, are worth exploring, with surprises at every turn. To the east is Timişoara's 18th-century **Bastion**, around which the city originally grew. Inside is the **Banat Ethnographical Museum** (Muzeul de Etnografie al Banatului; open Tues–Sun 10am–4.30pm; admission fee), which has reasonable exhibitions of traditional crafts and costumes, and an excellent gift shop.

South of Timişoara

Once the most fashionable place to take the waters in Central Europe, **Băile Herculane** (Hercules' Baths) is now a rather run-down resort in bad need of renovation. Arriving here by train is a pleasure, as the resort has one of Romania's most astonishing railway stations, with a brightly-coloured, tiled dome in the style of an extravagant Turkish bath. The resort remains popular with bathers, especially elderly Romanians, who claim its waters are a cure for almost anything. You

Romania's Atlantis

Located on the Danube about 3km (2 miles) downstream from Orşova, Ada Kaleh was a small island on which a mainly Turkish population of 4,000 people lived relatively independently of both Yugoslavia and Romania for much of the 20th century. On the island was an immense fortress, built by the Habsburgs in 1699 but the property of Turkey from 1738 until 1923, when the island's inhabitants voted to join Romania. The island disappeared under water in 1968 when the Iron Gates Dam was completed, but only after the fortress had been moved brick by brick to Simian Island, about 10km (6 miles) downstream. In 2005 Mehedinţi County Council announced it intended to restore the fortress fully, having been awarded an EU grant to do so. The work will continue for up to five years.

should not miss a chance to visit the astonishing **Iron Gates Dam** (Porțile de Fier) which towers above the Danube 10km (6 miles) west of the industrial town of Dobreta-Turnu Severin. The dam, built in the 1960s, is part of an enormous hydro-electrical complex that supplies much of Romania and Serbia's electricity.

The Museum of Arrested Thought in Sighet

Sighet

At the spiritual if not geographical heart of the enchanting Maramureş region, whose people are considered the most in-dependent-minded and strong-willed of all the Romanians, is Sighetu Marmaţiei, usually known just as **Sighet**. It is the northernmost town in Romania, almost on the Ukrainian border, and its remoteness is perhaps its most charming fea-ture. To get here you will either have to drive, or take a train from Cluj-Napoca (up to nine hours). Sighet should be your base for exploring the region, and you should begin with the city itself. The **Maramureş Museum** (Muzeul Maramureş-ului; open Tues–Sun 10am–6pm; admission fee) on Piaţa Libertăţii is the perfect introduction to the costumes, tradi-tions and rhythms of the Maramureş.

Sighet is infamous as the site of Romania's most secure prison, where the leading members of the inter-war aristo-cracy and political elite were held by the Communists. The prison on Piaţa Libertăţii is today the **Museum of Arrested Thought** (Muzeul al Gândirii Arestate; open daily 9.30am–6.30pm), Romania's best attempt yet to get to grips with its Communist past. The museum commemorates those who

Cheerful poems and paintings at the Merry Cemetery

died here, the very cream of Romanian intellectual and political society. Most died of starvation; others went mad in the tiny cells, where absolute silence was enforced 24 hours a day. It also commemorates all victims of Communism throughout Eastern Europe.

Sighet is also the birthplace of Elie Wiesel, the Jewish writer and Auschwitz survivor who allegedly first used the term 'Holocaust' with reference to World War II. Wiesel's house is on the corner of Str Dragos Voda and Tudor Vladimirescu, just north of Piața Libertății. Before World War II almost half the town's population was Jewish; most survived until 1944, when they were deported to Auschwitz. One synagogue (of eight) remains, on Str Bessarabia. A short drive west of Sighet is the village of **Săpânța**, famous for its **Merry Cemetery** (Cimitir Vesel), where all the crosses and headstones are brightly painted with happy scenes from the dead person's life.

East of Sighet, the **Iza Valley** is what the Maramureş is all about. Most of the valley lies in a natural park, and the houses and churches of the valley's villages have not changed for centuries. The area was so remote that much of the agricultural land was never collectivised by the Communist regime, so centuries-old traditions survive to this day. Many peasants still wear traditional local costume, especially on festival days. Your first stop in the valley should be **Vadu Izei**, where there is a Maramureş Information Centre (Fundatia OVR Agro-Tur). It is open year-round, and, as it is someone's house (Vadu Izei 161), there is usually someone there, night or day.

If you choose to explore the valley independently, you should stop at every village: all have something to see. At **Strâmtura** there is a wooden church from 1661, at **Rozavlea** a pine church from 1720, at **Sieu** a wooden church from 1760, and at **Poienile Izei** are the most obscene paintings you're ever likely to see in a church – frescos depicting the devil torturing (quite horribly) the sinful.

MOLDAVIA

Much of southern Moldavia is a vast plain of very little except dirt-poor villages and towns. There is not much of interest before **Iaşi**, a city of around 360,000 people close to the border with the Republic of Moldova, and a six-hour train journey from Bucharest. Long the most important city in Moldavia, Iaşi was the capital of Romania for two years during World War I, when the government and royal family decamped here for safety. A city with a great intellectual tradition, it is home to one of Romania's top universities.

Romanians call the region of Moldavia *Moldova*. When they refer to the country east of the river Prut (the Republic of Moldova), they will call it either *Republica Moldova* or *Bessarabia*.

The Hotel Traian in Iași was designed by Gustave Eiffel

The heart of Iași is **Piața Unirii**, though it is not a very picturesque heart. Central Iași suffered more rebuilding than most Romanian towns during the Communist years, and the monolithic Hotel Unirea which stands in the middle of Piața Unirii is testament to that. The glorious – though faded – neoclassical **Hotel Traian** immediately to the left is a reminder of how things used to be. It was completed in 1882 to a design by Gustave Eiffel, which indicates how important Iași was in the late 19th century.

Leading south from here is **Bulevardul Ștefan cel Mare si Sfant**, which must have been lovely once, but whose upper stretches are now lined with concrete blocks. However, there are three churches of note, all of which should be visited. The **Metropolitan Cathedral** (Catedrala Ortodoxă a Moldovei) is the first you will see, an enormous neoclassical church with superb interior paintings by the 19th-century realist Gheorghe Tatarescu. On 14 October the place is alive with tens of thousands of worshippers and pilgrims who flock to pay their respects at the remains of Moldavia's patron saint, Sfânta Cuvioasa Paraschiva, which lie in a silver casket to the side of the iconostasis.

A short distance further along Ştefan cel Mare is the rather ordinary **Roman Catholic Church** (Biserica Romano-Catolică), built in the late 1700s by Polish traders who at the time formed a large proportion of the city's population. Next to that is the city's finest church, the **Church of Three Saints** (Biserica Sf Trei Ierarhi), built 1637–41 in a neo-Byzantine style. The interior is as rich as any church in the country, all gold and brightly coloured frescos, with some striking marble tombs.

At the head of Bulevardul Ştefan cel Mare si Sfant is the most famous building in Iaşi, the **Palace of Culture** (Palatul Culturii). Built between 1906 and 1925, it was once the seat of the city's government and today houses four museums (open Tues–Sun 10am–4pm; admission fee). Only the **Art Museum** is at all interesting, home to a vast collection of works by Nicolae Grigorescu. The enormous equestrian statue in front of the building is of Ştefan cel Mare, considered the greatest of all Moldavian kings.

Statues of Moldavia's early rulers

The Painted Monasteries

Suceava, around 150km (90 miles) northwest of Iaşi, is a nice enough place, clean by Romanian standards and welcoming, but it would not be at all interesting to visitors were it not the gateway to the so-called painted

DRAGOS VODA   ALEXANDRU CEL BUN

monasteries of Moldavia. Once, long ago, the capital of Moldavia, Suceava does contain an extraordinary **Citadel** (Cetate de Scaun; open Tues–Sun 10am–5pm; admission fee) which overlooks the city from a steep hill to the south. The original citadel was built around 1390, and developed much further in the 1400s by Ştefan cel Mare, who fortified it with 33-metre (110-ft) high walls. Renovation work continues, though there is much to see, and children especially love clambering over the ramparts.

There are as many as 15 monasteries in the region around Suceava, but when referring to the famous painted monasteries, people usually mean the big five: Voroneţ, Humor,

The painted monastery of Moldoviţa

Moldoviţa, Suceviţa and Putna. Getting to the monasteries is impossible by public transport. You must either hire a car or join a monastery tour from Suceava. A number of companies arrange tours, including Icar Tours at 10 Vasile Alecsandri, Suceava <www.icartours.ro> and Marshal Turism <www.marshal.ro> in Bucharest, which arranges five-day pilgrimages to all of Moldavia's monasteries from the capital.

The monasteries were built and painted at a time when Moldavia was under constant threat from Turkish invasion. The idea of painting the outside walls was to inspire the illiterate Moldavian peasants who could not understand the Slavic liturgy going on inside. It would be foolish to even attempt to describe the beauty of the monasteries in any detail. It is enough to point the visitor in the right direction and let him or her stand in awe before these often coruscating wonders of the 15th and 16th centuries.

The most visited and famous is **Voroneţ** (open daily 8am–8pm; admission fee), a short drive southwest of Suceava. The *Last Judgement* fresco on its western wall is recognised as being the best of all the Moldavian paintings. The church was built in 1488 after Ştefan cel Mare had promised he would build a monastery if he were allowed to defeat the Turks. He was, and he kept his word.

Five kilometres (3 miles) north is **Humor** (open daily 9am–5pm; admission fee), built in 1530 with exterior paintings from 1535, including a violent though now much faded depiction of the 7th-century siege of Constantinople. Though always included in the same bracket as the monasteries, Humor is actually just a church, and has never been a monastery.

Northwest of Humor is the **Moldoviţa Monastery** (open daily 10am–6pm; admission fee), a fortified church in splendid grounds, whose exterior walls again depict the 626 siege of Constantinople. It was founded in 1532, and the frescos were painted the same year.

Some 30km (19 miles) northeast of Moldoviţa, along a precarious, winding mountain road is **Suceviţa** (open daily 9am–6pm; admission fee), the largest of the monasteries. Surrounded by an imposing fortress with four turrets, the main church was built from 1582 to 1600, and is entirely covered in frescos, from head to toe. The *Staircase of Virtue* mural on its northern wall depicts the 30 steps from Hell to Heaven, allegedly the journey taken by Orthodox monks on their deaths.

Even further north, almost at the Ukrainian border, is the fifth of the great monasteries, **Putna** (open daily 10am–6pm;

Romania's Favourite Poet

Mihai Eminescu (born Mihail Eminovici) was an outrageously handsome romantic poet, journalist and essayist whose tragic early death (he died in 1889 at the age of 38) sealed his place in Romania's artistic pantheon as the country's best-loved poet. Though his work is full of melancholy and longing, an overwhelming sense of hope flows from his poetry, not least in his epic work *Luceafărul (The Evening Star)*. Romanians study Eminescu throughout their school careers, and most can recite large chunks of his work.

Mountainous countryside near Bicaz, in the Eastern Carpathians

admission fee). Putna is semi-sacred to Romanians as the resting-place of Ştefan cel Mare, who built the monastery between 1466 and 1481. His tomb is below the church, alongside that of his wife and two of his children.

Piatra Neamţ to Vatra Dornei

You'll need to begin any trip to Piatra Neamţ and the natural wonders beyond at the ghastly industrial city that is **Bacău**. You should head straight through the city if possible, and head directly for **Piatra Neamţ**, which is a far nicer place 55km (34 miles) to the northwest. Neamţ County, of which Piatra Neamţ is the capital, is officially the poorest in Romania, but you would never know it walking around. The centre of the city surrounds Piaţa Libertăţii complete with obligatory statue of Ştefan cel Mare in the middle. Ignore the awful Hotel Ceahlău that towers over the square and concentrate instead on **St John's Church**

Submerged trees in Lacu Roşu

(Biserica Sfântului Ion), complete with its original 1499 watchtower.

However, the real reason the visitor comes to Neamţ County is to see the **Bicaz Gorge**, which cuts its way through limestone cliffs that are 300m (980ft) high in places. You'll find the narrowest points of the gorge, where the cliff literally overhangs the road and river below, about 20km (12 miles) beyond the small town of **Bicaz** itself. A short drive further on is the bizarre **Lacu Roşu** (Red Lake), formed in the 1830s when a landslide created a natural dam, and known for the protruding stumps of old fir trees that jut out of the water. The lake and small resort that has grown up around it are a good base for hiking in the **Ceahlău Massif** that overlooks them.

Head back to the town of Bicaz and take the northerly route along the side of the artificial **Lake Bicaz** (formed in 1950 by construction of the enormous dam at the lake's southern end), a stunning route of 120km (75 miles) through fantastic scenery, including more impressive gorges just past the village of Sunători. This route brings you to the resort town of **Vatra Dornei**. Vatra Dornei has long been known for its mineral water, which was drunk back in Roman times, and which is today the most popular mineral water in the country, sold under the brand name Dorna. A spa in Habsburg times, Vatra Dornei is today best-known as a ski resort.

THE DANUBE DELTA AND THE BLACK SEA

The Danube Delta is Romania's hidden treasure, a haven for a multitude of birds and wildlife. But the secret is getting out, as easier access and better accommodation see it begin to appear in Western holiday brochures. Most of the area is now protected by United Nations decree, after years of neglect and outright pillaging of nature during the latter part of the Communist period. Meanwhile, the resorts of the Black Sea coast, built with German investment in the late 1960s, are once again attracting international tourists after a barren decade.

The Danube Delta

The capital of the Delta region, **Tulcea**, is an industrial town with little charm and very little to see. If you are keen on seeing the Delta, however, the chances are you will pass

Boatmen on the backwaters of the Danube Delta

There are daily ferry services on all the branches of the Delta

through here, and you may have to spend at least a night. All of the Navrom ferries for the villages of the Delta depart from here, and there are several agencies which organise specialist tours. If you want to see the Delta properly, we recommend joining one of these tours *(see page 125)*. Independent travel can be time-consuming and trying on the patience.

The Delta is split into three channels: the Chilia Channel, which runs from Tulcea along the Ukrainian border to Periprava; the Sulina Channel, which runs from Tulcea to Sulina; and the Sfantu Gheorghe Channel, which runs from Tulcea to Sfantu Gheorghe. The ferry company Navrom has daily services along all three channels, stopping at the various villages along the way. If time is short, it is a good idea simply to join one of these ferries and take it to the end of the line and back. You will get a good introduction to Delta life (including an idea of how remote the area is), as well as seeing a good range of wildlife. If you want to explore the

Delta's backwaters, you must join an organised tour or simply hire a boat from a fisherman. The main reason people come to the Delta is to birdwatch. Home to over 300 species, the Danube Delta is a dream for ornithologists. For details of birdwatching in the Delta *see page 84.*

Constanţa

In summer Romania's second-largest city, **Constanţa**, is a hot, dusty place that is unavoidable if you are heading to any of Romania's coastal resorts. Constanţa has been around in one form or another since around 600BC, first as a small Greek settlement called Tomis, and later as the Roman port of Pontus Sinister. It was the Byzantines who christened the city Constanţa in the 6th century AD. Modern Constanţa is one of Europe's largest working ports. There are oil refineries in the region, too, making the city one of the wealthiest in Romania.

Despite all the heavy industry, Constanţa is a popular holiday resort in its own right, for it has a splendid beach and much to see, mainly its ancient walls, relics and the museums that house them. Start off in the heart of Old Tomis, at **Piaţa Ovidiu** (named after the Roman poet Ovid, who was exiled to Mamaia; a statue of him stands in the middle of the square) and its spacious, informative **Museum of National History and Archaeology** (Muzeul de Istorie Naţională si Arheolgie; open Tues–Sun 10am–4pm; admission fee). Just behind the museum are the remnants of a stunning **Roman mosaic** (Tues–Sun 10am–6pm; admission fee) discovered in 1959.

A short walk south of Piaţa Ovidiu is the more impressive of Constanţa's two working mosques, the **Mahmudiye Mosque**, whose 55-m (180-ft) minaret is open to visitors (Tues–Thur, Sat–Sun 10am–5pm). The vast and somewhat subdued **Romanian Orthodox Cathedral** (Catedrala Ortodoxă), completed in 1895, is only slightly further on, and 100m or so beyond that lies the seafront.

It's enjoyable enough just walking along here, as the promenade is wide and inviting, and during the evening there is quite a procession of courting couples and families with children. There is a disappointing **Aquarium** (open Tues–Sun 9am–6pm; admission fee) on the left-hand side of the prom, with the much photographed and rather over-the-top **Casino** opposite. The casino was built in 1909, when Constanţa was one of Europe's leading seaside resorts. It no longer welcomes gamblers, but is immensely popular with high rollers who rent it for wedding parties and christenings. Just beyond the casino is a **lighthouse**, an 1860 replica of an earlier 15th-century construction.

Constanţa's grand casino

North of Piaţa Ovidiu is the **Folk Art Museum** (Muzeul de Artă Populara; open Tues–Sun 10am–6pm), a good but not extraordinary collection of traditional costumes and handicrafts housed in a somewhat out-of-place Turkish-style building, with the city's other, less impressive mosque opposite.

A short walk from here brings you to the **Archaeology Park** (Parcul Arheologic), named after the fragments of 3rd-century Roman city wall that runs through it, and a number of other relics, including a Byzantine-era bastion known as the Butchers' Tower. The dull Victory Monument in front of it is a

1968 aberration. The city's **Town Hall** (Prefectura) is the large building that splits the park in two.

Just south of the park, in lovely grounds, is the **Romanian Navy Museum** (Muzeul Marinei Române; open Tues–Sun 9am–5pm; admission fee), with interesting though haphazardly arranged exhibits chronicling the history not just of the Romanian navy but of sailing in the Black Sea region in general. Heading north along Bulevardul Tomis, Constanța's main commercial street, there are shops, cafés and restaurants, with a number of half-decent terraces on Str Ştefan cel Mare, the city's one pedestrianised street.

Mamaia

The only sign that Constanța's suburbs have given way to the beach resort of **Mamaia** is the security barrier that marks the resort's entrance.

Mamaia is located on a narrow strip of land that stretches 3km (2 miles) or so, separating Lake Siutghiol from the Black Sea. It was Romania's first real seaside resort, and though for much of the 1980s Neptun was considered more fashionable and exclusive, Mamaia is now once again the best and most expensive resort in the country.

Mamaia's biggest attraction is its wide, sandy beach that slopes slowly into the sea. There are hundreds of places to partake in watersports – but make sure you have good insurance, as many of these concessions will not. At the resort's entrance there is an enormous outdoor **water park** (open

Hotels in Mamaia come in all shapes and sizes, from ordinary two-star places to the enormous five-star Rex. For the best prices you should make sure you book in advance through an agency, as turning up on spec can be expensive, and in August outright impossible because most hotels are full.

8am–10pm May–Sep; admission fee) and to the north of that is the entrance to Mamaia's **gondola lift** (telegondola; 9am–10pm May–Oct; admission fee). A typical ski-lift gondola, it takes visitors from one end of the resort to the other in about eight minutes, offering great views of the lake to one side and the Black Sea to the other. As darkness falls Mamaia lives up to its reputation as the summer nightlife capital of Romania, with plenty of discos to keep the crowds happy.

South of Constanţa

South of Constanţa there is a whole gaggle of beach resorts, all built in the 1960s to cater for Western tourists. However, the first point of interest on the road south is the mouth of the **Danube–Black Sea Canal**. This costly folly is not in fact the original Black Sea Canal, known as the Canal of Death, which was abandoned in 1953 after thousands of political prisoners had died attempting to drive a canal through to a point on the Black Sea close to Navodări. The project was resurrected in 1975 by Ceauşescu, and a new route was dug, this time by some of the highest-paid workers in the country. It opened in 1984, but little traffic ever uses it.

The resorts of **Eforie Nord** and **Eforie Sud** are known for their mud treatments. A number of public treatment centres can be found along the banks of Lake Techirghiol, and for a small fee you can cover yourself in the thick black mud that is said to cure everything from rheumatism to varicose veins.

The next resort along the coast is **Costineşti**, for years the students' favourite. Today it is popular with families, who stay in the hundreds of private villas behind the beach. The beaches here are especially well kept, though a little narrow. Next is the twin resort of **Neptun-Olimp**, the most exclusive

Neptun-Olimp was once Romania's most exclusive resort

place in Romania during the 1980s. To get a hotel reservation here you had to know very important people or have a lot of money, or usually both. Today the showpiece hotel on the beachfront, the Amfiteatru, is a run-down place that shows little sign of its glorious past.

The resorts of **Jupiter**, **Cap-Aurora**, **Saturn** and **Venus** are all very much the same, full of drab hotels for Romanian package tourists. The town of **Mangalia** is a pleasant enough place with a good beach, but as dull as ditchwater.

From here you can drive or hitch-hike to Romania's once bohemian resorts **Doi Mai** and **Vama Veche**. Both used to attract a laid-back student crowd, were popular with hippies, and had few if any facilities. Most people simply pitched tents on the beach. All that has changed since the early 2000s. A construction boom has seen large numbers of loud terraces, beach bars and guesthouses spring up in both resorts, bringing in a more mainstream crowd.

WHAT TO DO

SPORTS

Thanks to its highly varied natural landscape, Romania is an excellent place to take part in many outdoor sports. The mountainous regions provide an ideal arena for skiing and hiking, and the abundant and diverse wildlife, particularly in the Danube Delta region, means that opportinities for hunting, fishing and birdwatching are plentiful.

Skiing

Skiiing is popular in Romania, though the experience can often be a less than satisfactory one. The country's main resort is Poiana Braşov, a short drive from the city of Braşov *(see page 42)*. It has long been a favourite with package holidaymakers, who in the past often had the resort to themselves. Now it buzzes – especially at the weekend – with the new Romanian rich, who flock here in large numbers. Queues for the cable-cars on Saturday and Sunday can be very long. However, during the week, you may well find the slopes empty. A day's skiing here can cost as much as €30.

Besides Poiana Braşov there are two other very popular ski resorts: Sinaia *(see page 45)* and Predeal *(see page 43)*. Both are well blessed with hotels and places to hire ski equipment. Snow can usually be guaranteed from the beginning of December until the end of March; the highest slopes at Sinaia often stay open as late as mid-May.

There are other skiing options in Romania, notably in the north at Borşa and Vatra Dornei, at Paltiniş near Sibiu, and at Semenic near Craiova, but none of these has more than one or two ski runs.

Walkers in the Bicaz Gorge

Hiking and Walking

Hiking is probably the most popular activity in Romania. The season begins in June, as the unpredictable mountain weather makes hiking any earlier dangerous. The most popular areas for hiking are the Bucegi and Făgăraş ranges, where hundreds of well-marked routes of all levels and lengths crisscross the mountains. A network of *cabane* – basic mountain huts with bunk beds and hot food – provide overnight shelter to the legions of local and international hikers who head for the hills every summer. Camping in the mountains is not a good idea, as bears, boars and foxes can be a danger.

For gentler walks as opposed to hikes, Poiana Braşov and Predeal are perfect bases for exploring the countryside. Both have cable transport to take you up to the mountains, from where you can enjoy sensational views, before gently walking down to the resort.

Hunting

You may hunt a wide variety of wildlife in Romania, including ducks, geese, wild boars, lynx, stags and even bears, though under very strict conditions. Hunting is expensive, as you will have to pay trophy fees depending on the size of your prey. There are limits to the number of each species that can be shot, and poaching is punishable with heavy prison sentences.

If you want to hunt in Romania, you must have an international firearms licence and hunting-liability insurance. ONT, the former state tourist agency, can arrange custom-made hunting tours throughout the country, and help with formalities, including the importation of firearms (hunters may import two guns and 100 cartridges). ONT in Bucharest can be found at 7 Bulevardul General Magheru; tel: 021-314 51 60. Their website (in English) is <www.ont.ro>. Marshal Turism (43 Bulevardul Maghreu; tel: 021-319 44 55; <www.marshal. ro>) also offers hunting trips throughout Romania.

Fishing from a ferry in the Danube Delta

Fishing

Fishing is popular throughout the country. Freshwater fishing is especially good in the Apuseni Mountains, where you will be able to find carp, mullet, pike and pike-perch, depending on the season. Only May (the spawning season) is off-limits to anglers. But the Danube Delta is the best fishing destination, with a number of local fishermen offering trips that can last for days, staying at remote pensions or private houses in some of the best countryside in Romania. Huge carp are the prime attraction here, though you can fish for catfish and pike too.

The Black Sea offers huge numbers of saltwater fish, including turbot, mackerel and tuna. More adventurous types should note that the small dog shark can be fished from a boat around four kilometres off the coast.

Most Bucharest tour agencies can help fix you up with angling trips.

Birdwatching

The Danube Delta is home to over 300 species of bird, and birdwatching in the region is one of the fastest-growing areas of Romanian tourism. The best times of year are April–May and September–October, though many wintering species can be seen throughout the year. Dalmatian pelicans, white pelicans (Europe's largest breeding colony), swans, ibis, egrets, herons, spoonbills, larks, starlings and many others live in the Delta all year round, while redstarts, black woodpeckers, penduline tits, pygmy cormorants and white-tailed eagles can be seen in migration.

Pelicans on the Delta

Many areas of the Delta are protected, and getting around can be difficult, so even experienced birdwatchers will get far more from a trip by joining an organised tour. Specialist birdwatching tours are organised in Romania by Liscom Tour, 13 Str Viitorului, Tulcea; tel: 0240-53 67 26; <www.turismdelta.ro>. Liscom operates its own luxury boat-hotel, and offers tours ranging from one night to a week. Less salubrious but no less interesting tours are also organised by Ibis Travel, 1 Str Griviței, Tulcea; tel: 0240-51 27 87.

Football

Romanians are crazy about football, though recently there has been very little to celebrate. The national side has not gone far in a major championship since 1994, and a dearth of talent means they could be out of the international limelight for some time. The stars the country produces tend to play abroad, mainly in Spain, Italy and Turkey; although the standard of the local league (Divizia A) is poor by European standards, it still has a pull among fans, and big games are well worth attending.

It is a long time since Steaua Bucharest won the European Cup (1986), but they remain the country's biggest club, and local derbies with rivals Dinamo Bucharest and Rapid Bucharest draw big crowds. Tickets are hard to obtain via normal channels, though their relatively low face-value (from 3 lei upwards) means you should be able to pick one up from a tout outside the stadiums for as little as 50 lei. The best-supported teams in the country are in fact Politechnica Timişoara and Universitatea Craiova: crowds here can top 30,000.

Steaua plays its home matches at Ghencea Stadium, Bulevardul Ghencea. The national team plays most of its home games at the National Stadium in Bucharest, close to Piaţa Muncii metro station.

SHOPPING

While it would be an exaggeration to state that Romania is the shopping capital of Europe, there is still plenty to buy here. This is in marked contrast to the Communist period, when shops stood empty, and Romanians queued endlessly for even the most basic foodstuffs. Today, modern malls and shopping centres heave daily with thousands of shoppers looking for the latest in Western fashion and hi-tech

Traditional lace is a good buy

equipment (Romanians are mad about gadgets of all kinds; there are no less than four monthly magazines dedicated to the latest gadgets). As you would expect, Bucharest has the widest range of stores, though huge malls also now make Constanța, Brașov, Iași and Arad reasonable places to shop. Most things, especially clothes, electronics and books will cost far more than in Western Europe. For bargains you will need to stick to locally produced items. Leather shoes are a good buy.

Where to Shop

Bucharest's main shopping districts are Calea Victoriei, where you will find high-end brand names such as Max Mara, Clinique, Pal Zileri, etc, and Bulevardul General Magheru, home to more reasonably priced retail outlets.

For souvenirs try the excellent shop in the National Peasant Museum. The Lipscani area is home to innumerable

Souvenir stalls in the Old Town, Sighișoara

pawn shops, textile emporia, antiques dealers and small art galleries.

In Braşov, the centre of the city around Piaţa Sfatului has a number of good little shops, notably art and antiques outlets. Second-hand book stores line Str Mureşenilor, while cut-price ski equipment can often be bought from a number of shops in the city centre. There is a large, modern shopping mall slightly out of town on the road to Râşnov.

> Romania is alone in Eastern Europe in not having any real flea markets, though on the central streets of many cities you will find shady characters selling copies of the latest CDs, DVDs and computer games.

Markets and Malls

Bucharest has three enormous shopping malls: Unirea, the Bucureşti Mall and Plaza Romania. Unirea, in Piaţa Unirii, is the most interesting, as it was for many years the showpiece department store of Communist Romania, full of hundreds of items that nobody wanted to buy, and very little that they actually did. Today it is a hotchpotch of hundreds of shops and stores for all pockets, with a food hall in the basement.

The Bucureşti Mall and Plaza Romania are far more modern malls, full of trendy and (for local pockets) expensive shops. Their multi-levels contain restaurants, children's play areas and multiplex cinemas. There are similar malls in Oradea, Iaşi, Braşov and Constanţa.

Romania's markets are fantastic. Produce is almost entirely organic, cheap and fresh. Prices are low, and vegetables in this part of the world have real flavour. Most produce is still strictly seasonal, though imported goods can be found in the nation's supermarkets. Romania has a thriving textile industry, and produces clothes for many big-name brands. Many seconds and copies find their way into Bucharest's fashion markets.

The city's best markets are Piaţa Amzei, which is situated between Bulevardul General Magheru and Calea Victoriei, and Piaţa Obor, which you can reach by metro (alight at Obor). The enormous Obor market covers 16 city blocks with open and covered stalls selling anything from CDs to pots and pans to live chickens.

The Local Wine

Romanian wine is respected by connoisseurs the world over for its consistently high quality and good value, but it is not as well known or marketed as its Bulgarian counterpart. There are eight main wine-producing regions: Moldavia, Muntenia, Oltenia, Dobrogea, Ardeal, Banat, Crisan and Maramureş. Moldavia is by far the largest producer, accounting for more than a third of all Romanian wine. It is famous for the sweet dessert wines of the Cotnari label – the Tamaioasa Românească wine is splendid – and the fruity reds of Odobeşti.

The southern regions of Muntenia and Oltenia are dominated by the Cabernet Sauvignon, Merlot and Pinot Noir grapes used in Dealul Mare wines from the Prahova Valley. Murfatlar is the dominant producer in Dobrogea, and is probably the best-known Romanian brand internationally. It bottles excellent Chardonnay, while also turning out classic Pinot Noir and Cabernet Sauvignon. A famous dessert wine, Lacrima lui Ovidiu (Ovid's Tears), is also produced in Dobrogea. Târnave, which produces fruity white wines, is the dominant label of Transylvania.

There are a number of specialist wine merchants in Bucharest, Braşov, Timişoara and Iaşi. Many wineries offer tours of their vineyards and cellars. The Cotnari region, close to Iaşi, Murfatlar, close to Constanţa, and Dealul Mare, not too far from Bucharest, are the most accessible.

What to Buy

Traditional Romanian handicrafts worth looking out for include lace, pottery, wood carvings and iconography. Romanian souvenir shops are ubiquitous, though the souvenirs themselves can be patchy in quality.

Reproductions of Orthodox iconography and wood carvings can be found all over the country, with the best quality being found in Bucharest, in some of the little shops in Hanul cu Tei *(see page 27)*. As a rule, the goods sold by hawkers and stallholders outside the more famous Romanian sights and monasteries should be purchased only in a souvenir

Romanian pottery is still mainly made by hand, thrown on a wheel

emergency, as quality is mediocre at best. An exception is the excellent craft market at the foot of Bran Castle.

If you are after genuine antique icons as opposed to reproductions, you should contact a professional art dealer and have a reasonable idea of what you are looking for. Exporting antiques is a difficult process requiring a long paper-chase that a dealer will be able to handle for you. Only the brave should attempt to do it on their own. There are a number of galleries in Bucharest, clustered together on the streets around the Lipscani area and in the National Theatre.

Intricate embroidery and lace can be found in good souvenir shops, and the one at the National Peasant Museum in

Bucharest is especially well stocked. The craft markets at Bran Castle and on the road between Sinaia and Predeal are also worth exploring for high-quality work, though don't expect bargains: prices for such painstaking work are high.

There are various other unique souvenirs that make great presents from Romania. The country recently developed its own version of Monopoly, using the streets and squares of Bucharest. It can be found in most toyshops and costs around 110 lei. Replica painted Easter eggs also make super gifts.

ENTERTAINMENT AND FESTIVALS

Traditional Music

The origins of what today we term Romanian folk music are convoluted and disputed; it is at times very difficult to differentiate between traditional Serb, Romanian, Bulgar-

Traditional music and dancing in Braşov

ian and Macedonian music. The central element of traditional music is the *doină*, a long, often unscripted love song, usually sung by a female and telling of lost love or longing. The Romanian notion of *dor* (in the sense that something is missed so much that it affects reason) is widespread in the country's folk music. You are most likely to hear *doine* in the countryside, as the kind of folk music you will hear in the capital and in tourist centres is likely to be a diluted, tourist-friendly version far from the emotion of the real thing.

For a real taste of Romanian music you are in fact far better off listening to a Gypsy band, a *taraf*, whose own music is much faster and more rhythmic than its traditional Romanian counterpart. *Tarafe* are increasingly popular, and many restaurants have a resident *taraf* performing most evenings, often accompanied by a rather kitsch *program folcloric*.

Opera

There are major opera houses in Bucharest, Timişoara, Cluj-Napoca and Constanţa, with smaller opera houses in Braşov and Iaşi. Cluj-Napoca also has a Hungarian Opera. Opera has a long history in Romania, and it is enjoyed by a surprisingly wide variety of people, of all ages. Most opera houses offer a standard repertoire of well-known operas, and tickets are usually remarkably cheap. The season runs from October to May, though touring operas often perform out of season in open-air theatres at the Black Sea. The Romanian Opera's website is <www.operanb.ro>.

Classical Music

Even more than opera, classical-music concerts attract large and enthusiastic crowds all over Romania. However, the best place to enjoy classical music is at the Ateneu Roman in

Bucharest, a sublime building *(see page 33)* with outstanding acoustics. Concerts are held here almost every night, and tickets are relatively cheap.

Romania's national composer is George Enescu. His best known work is the astonishing *Romanian Rhapsody*, written while he was living in Paris in 1901. He was just 20 at the time. The Bucharest Philharmonic Orchestra, created as long ago as 1777, is based at the Ateneu Roman, and now carries his name.

Nightlife

Before 1990, nightlife didn't really exist in Romania. Tawdry cabarets and discos full of prostitutes catered to foreign package tourists in Poiana Braşov and at the seaside, though even here the lights would often go out at 10pm due to power cuts. All that changed very quickly after the revolution. Bucharest today is one of Europe's best clubbing destinations, and the Black Sea resort of Mamaia parties from May to September with almost no pause. Every town has its trendy bars and clubs, as well as

---

Top of the Pops

One distinctly Romanian style of music you may come across is *muzică populară* (literally: pop music), which is a fusion of the traditional *doină* and Gypsy rhythms. During the Communist era, when much Western rock music was banned, *muzică populară* was about all there was. However, far more popular at the moment are *manele*, a turbo-folk concoction of traditional folk, Turkish melodies and Gypsy rhythms. Popular all over the Balkans, *manele* and their practitioners, *manelişti*, are adored and idolised in Romania. Subjects for songs never go far beyond *parai* (money) and *fete* (girls). You will not escape Romania without hearing a fair amount of *manele*.

Casinos are big business in Bucharest and elsewhere in Romania

a more lurid side too: casinos and strip joints are big business everywhere in Romania.

Its sheer size makes Bucharest the country's leading nightlife spot, and there is an endless choice of pubs, clubs and discos. The trendiest place in the country is probably The Office (2 Str Tache Ionescu), while Coyote Café (48–50 Calea Victoriei; tel: 021-311 34 87) is a lively music club, with live bands every night. Kristal Club (2 Str J.S. Bach) hosts Europe's biggest-name DJs every Friday and Saturday night. But the nightlife scene in Bucharest – as in any city – is notoriously fickle, and things do change. The excellent *Bucharest In Your Pocket* guide has listings of all the best clubs. You should also check the website <www.nights.ro> for the latest news on the Romanian club scene.

Jazz is big all over Romania, and every major city has at least one jazz club. Sibiu is the country's jazz capital, and the city hosts an international jazz festival every May.

Easter Rituals

As in much of the Orthodox world, Easter is a far more sacred event in Romania than Christmas, and it can be a very good time to visit the country and observe the many rituals of the holiday. Lent, of course, leads up to Easter, with a large number of Romanians observing the fast and its incumbent restrictions: meat, fish and dairy products are not eaten, while weddings and christenings are forbidden. Palm Sunday (one week before Easter Sunday) is known in Romania as *Florilor* (Flower Day), and you will see people carrying holy willow away from church, having had it blessed by passing it over an icon.

From noon on Good Friday until Saturday night the pious fast completely, before going to church to attend midnight mass. Churches are usually so full that large crowds have to stand outside and hear the service relayed by loudspeaker.

Hard-boiled eggs are elaborately painted for Easter

Everyone will be holding a candle. At exactly midnight a priest will appear with a flame, and announce that *Hristos a înviat* (Christ has risen). The flame is passed from person to person and the candles are lit. People

In some parts of Romania egg painting has become an elaborate art form. You can find exquisite painted (wooden) eggs in many gift shops

then make their way home, ensuring the candle remains alight. The Easter meal of lamb – the only time of year the animal is eaten – is then served. Romanians precede the meal by knocking painted hard-boiled eggs against each other, and declaring again that 'Christ has risen'. The meal can last until the early hours of Sunday morning, when people return to church to collect *pasti* – holy bread and wine.

CHILDREN'S ROMANIA

Romania offers plenty of thrills for children, and they will be made to feel especially welcome wherever in the country you take them. The main problem with travelling with children in Romania is the poor transport infrastructure that makes getting from one town to another difficult and time-consuming. Try to plan your travel well.

The ski resort of Poiana Braşov has specialist children's ski schools, ice rinks, gentle slopes for sledging, and swimming pools. There are also horse-drawn sleigh rides through the snow from the resort's equestrian centre. In summer the same place organises children's riding courses and pony trekking. It really is a great destination for active children. Predeal too has a special children's ski slope, and a winter playground in front of the resort's Town Hall.

In the summer the resort of Mamaia has a fantastic water park, as well as a gondola ride which offers great views of the resort and the sea. The beach at Mamaia is tremendous:

wide, sandy and perfect for children. Most of Romania's other beaches are less child-friendly.

The capital is not a great destination for children, though there is a water park just outside the city, opposite the airport. Bucharest also has a zoo, and plenty of playgrounds in its large parks. In Herăstrău Park there are pleasure boats which cruise around the large lake, as well as a go-kart track for older children, and Insula Copiilor (Children's Island) – all bouncy castles, slides and other inflatables. If it rains, take the kids to Arlechino Club at 9 B-dul Unirii, a large indoor playground. There is a very good circus in the capital at 15 Aleea Circului, with shows every Saturday and Sunday at 3pm and 6.30pm. Tickets are cheap.

The water park at Mamaia

When it comes to eating out with children, you will find that few restaurants turn them away, though equally few are actually well prepared for them. High chairs are rare, except in the best hotels and international chain restaurants, like Pizza Hut and Ruby Tuesday. Public baby-changing facilities are also very difficult to find. Food in general should not be a problem. Romanians themselves are not fond of spicy foods, while universal children's favourites, such as omelettes or steak with fries, are to be found on every menu. And McDonald's is ubiquitous.

Calendar of Events

1 January New Year is celebrated all over the country by groups of young men who wander through cities and villages in goatskins, sheepskins and even bearskins singing, dancing and banging drums, collecting money from onlookers.

1 March All females are presented with a *mărţişor* – usually a brooch tied with red-and-white thread – which symbolises the coming of spring.

8 March International Women's Day, celebrated in Romania by men giving women flowers.

April Orthodox Easter – which falls according to the Gregorian calendar – is the most important event of the year *(see page 94 for more details)*.

May/June The Sibiu Jazz Festival has been a fixture on the international jazz calendar since 1970. It attracts top international names, as well as the cream of Romania's jazz scene.

June Juni Festival in Braşov (first Sunday). The Transylvania Film Festival, held in Cluj-Napoca every June, showcases new Romanian cinema.

21 June Concerts in Bucharest celebrate the Fête de la Musique, part of a worldwide international Francophile music festival.

July Sighişoara Medieval Arts Festival: a three-day event with pop and rock concerts, handicraft exhibitions, craft fairs and street theatre.

July or September Cerbul de Aur (Carpathian Stag) Pop Festival in Piaţa Sfatului, Braşov.

Late August Mamaia Music Festival, a Romanian copy of the Italian San Remo contest, held in an open-air arena

September George Enescu Music Festival, the country's most important cultural event, held on odd-numbered years over 10 days at the Ateneu Roman in Bucharest.

1 December National Day celebrates the unification of Transylvania with Wallachia and Moldavia. Usually a military parade in Bucharest and a religious service at Alba Iulia (where the unification treaty was signed).

24 December Carol-singing is enormously popular on Christmas Eve.

31 December Almost every town holds open-air New Year's Eve concerts, regardless of the weather. The biggest is in Bucharest at Piaţa Revoluţiei.

EATING OUT

Romania does not distinguish itself by the quality, range or inventiveness of its cuisine. Many of the country's most famous dishes will be familiar to the traveller who has visited Turkey, Bulgaria or the former Yugoslavia, only under slightly different names. The best of Romanian food is usually eaten in family homes, where you can be sure that only the freshest and the best ingredients have been used. Many Romanian restaurants cut corners and prepare sub-standard dishes that do not fully represent the best of Romania.

There are, of course, exceptions – not least Coliba Haiducilor in Poiana Braşov, the country's most famous Romanian restaurant – and you should not be concerned about being able to eat well in Romania. Every town has at least two or three excellent eateries, and Bucharest and Braşov have several restaurants of the highest international standard. Vegetarians are less lucky, as voluntarily going without meat is still considered a bizarre habit in these parts.

> **Restaurants in Romania usually open for lunch around 11am and stay open until late at night. They rarely close during the afternoon.**

Asian and Middle Eastern restaurants in Bucharest cater to vegetarians, but in the countryside you may be restricted to egg and chips, even then only to discover that they were cooked in the fat of an animal. All this is strange, as Romanian cuisine does have a number of vegetarian specialities, including *borş de lobodă* (sour soup), rice-stuffed peppers, *iahnie de fasole* (bean stew) and fried courgettes with cheese. They just seldom appear on restaurant menus, and a good Romanian hostess would feel she was insulting her guest if she did not serve them hearty portions of meat. The only time you can find vegetarian food widely available is during *post* (Lent). Look out for the sign *Avem produse de post.*

Romanians tend to eat very early, light breakfasts – often just coffee with bread, cheese and salami – followed by an early lunch of quite considerable proportions. Until recently lunch was the primary meal of the day, and even today evening meals are often an afterthought, eaten late. The main Easter meal is taken after midnight mass on Saturday night/Sunday morning. Such meals, especially in large families, can often go on all night.

WHAT TO EAT

The Romanian staple is pork *(porc)*, and it is simply superb. You will find it served in a variety of ways, though to sample its succulent flavour and smooth texture a steak, grilled on an open fire, is the best. It is also very good when

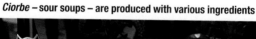

Ciorbe – sour soups – are produced with various ingredients

roasted on the bone and served with *iahnie de fasole*. The dish is called *ciolan de porc cu fasole*.

Chicken *(pui)* in Romania is equally common, though nowhere near as good in quality. Beef *(vita)* is also common but usually unreliable, often poor, and most beef served in good restaurants will be imported. Lamb *(miel)* is common only at Easter, when it forms the basis of the Easter meal.

In the Danube Delta you will come across game, notably duck and geese, and around Braşov you will find boar and even bear steaks on the menu.

A cheese seller in Baia Mare in the Maramureş region

With a not insignificant coastline and innumerable inland lakes and waterways, you would expect Romania to be a fish-loving country. It isn't. Carp *(crap)* is eaten occasionally, usually grilled and simmered in a sour sauce called *saramură*, as is trout *(pastrav)* and pike-perch *(salau)*. And that's about it. There are several seafood restaurants in Bucharest, but they serve exclusively imported fish at inflated prices.

Romanian bread *(pâine)* can be disappointing, as it is made cheaply using often poor flour, but don't forgo *covrigi* – plain bread bagels sold on street corners everywhere, covered in salt and delicious when piping hot.

Popular Dishes

Romanians claim many dishes as their own, only for the visitor to find the same thing all over the Balkans. The nation's most famous dish is unquestionably *sarmale cu mamaligă*, cabbage leaves stuffed with minced pork and rice and served with polenta. It is usually found on the menus of traditional Romanian restaurants, and is eaten by the whole country at Christmas.

Romania is famous for its *ciorbe* – sour soups. Try *ciorbă de burta* (tripe soup) or *ciorbă de perişoare* (meatball soup). Another popular delicacy is *vinete*, a salad made from grilled aubergines and served spread on bread. Aubergines are also popular grilled and served pickled in oil and vinegar.

Transylvanian specialities include *tocaniţa*, a stew of chicken, pork or beef, cooked slowly for hours in a hotpot with generous amounts of paprika, betraying the enduring Hungarian influence on the region.

A Feast of Vegetables

Romania's best culinary assets are its superb fruit and vegetables, which are strictly seasonal and have real flavour. Though agricultural techniques are slowly adopting Western European methods, much produce remains organic. Tomatoes especially have a taste that long ago disappeared from supermarkets in Western Europe. Sweetcorn *(porumb)* is popular in season (August and early September), and you will find street vendors selling boiled cobs all over the country. Melons, both water *(pepene)* and honeydew *(pepene galben)*, are fabulous, and appear at the end of July. Prices are high at the beginning of the season, but by the end of September they are all but given away. New potatoes *(cartofi noi)* are stunning from May to July, and fresh cabbage *(varza)* will change your perception of that vegetable.

When it comes to dessert, Romanians have a very sweet tooth. It is the Turkish influence that is strongest here. *Baclava* is common, especially in Wallachia, while *cozonac*, sweet bread with chocolate or raisins, is eaten by everyone at Easter and Christmas, but enjoyed all year round. *Clatite cu brânza* are crêpes filled with cottage cheese, raisins and spices.

Romanians also love *gogoşi* – plain doughnuts, served hot and crispy with *smântană* (sour cream). *Papanaşi* are smaller doughnuts, usually filled with jam. You will also come across *plăcinte*, fried pies stuffed with jam or cheese and topped with sour cream. They are best eaten piping hot.

WHERE TO EAT

It took many years after 1989 before Romania really began to get serious about eating out. As late as 1998, there were few places where you could eat well anywhere in the country. Since then there has been a veritable explosion of restaurants, though variety and quality remains patchy. Restaurants serving good Romanian food are still hard to find, though there are a couple of note in Bucharest, Sinaia, Predeal, Braşov, Poiana Braşov, Sibiu and Cluj-Napoca.

You should not leave Romania without tasting *mici* – small, spicy, sausage-shaped meatballs (a mixture of pork and mutton) grilled on an open fire and served with bread and mustard. Though found all over Romania, they are best in the south, in Wallachia. The smell of *mici* cooking is common in markets and on terraces, and is impossible to resist.

Some places have an evening folklore show (usually of questionable taste), or Gypsy fiddlers going from table to table. Prices, even at the best Romanian restaurants, are usually low.

Perla Maramuresului restaurant in the ski resort of Borsa

However, for a real taste of Romania, and to be sure of great food, you should try to get yourself invited to a Romanian home. The food will not stop coming until you insist convincingly enough that you can eat no more. If you do find yourself invited to a home, make sure you take flowers for your hostess.

Cosmopolitan Bucharest offers restaurants of every cuisine imaginable, from Japanese to Indian to the latest in cutting edge French-Asian Fusion. However, prices can be surprisingly high – which is perhaps understandable, given that many ingredients are imported.

Braşov, Timişoara and Cluj-Napoca are also blessed with a variety of restaurants. The one place in Romania where it can be tough to get a decent meal is on the Black Sea coast, where most visitors eat in their hotels, with meals usually included in their packages. Wherever you are in Romania, though, you will not starve. There is always somewhere serving a simple steak and chips.

WHAT TO DRINK

Now the good news. Romania is a wine-and-beer-producing country, and prices are rock-bottom. Romania has been producing wine since Dacian times and has eight major wine-producing regions. Do not miss the wines of the Cotnari label, especially the Tamaioasa Romaneasca dessert wine, or any wine on the Château Domenii label.

Among the population at large, however, beer is far more popular than wine. Romania's best beers are Timişoreana, Ciuc, Aurora, Burger and Tuborg. All are now owned by large international brewery companies, thus ensuring consistent high quality. Romanian beers are usually light, more like Western lager. If you want something stronger, ask for a *berea neagră*, dark beer, more like the English bitter. The Aurora brewery in Braşov produces a particularly good

Bar expertise at Bucharest's top hotel, the Athenee Palace Hilton

berea neagră, called Aurora Neagră. Imported beers are also widely available, and popular among the urban elite.

The local spirit is *ţuică*, and its slightly more refined counterpart *pălincă*. Both are made with plums or cherries, and are extremely strong. The taste, once you are used to it, can be surprisingly good. Though they are produced and sold commercially, the home-made variety is far better. Most Romanians have a family member in the countryside who can procure them the genuine article.

Romanian tap water is safe to drink, but there are a huge number of springs dotted throughout the country, which makes bottled water cheap and plentiful.

To Help You Order...

Can I see the menu?	**Puteţi să mi arătaţi meniul?**
I'm a vegetarian	**Sunt vegetarian (m)**
	vegetariană (f)
Can I have a beer, please	**Aş vrea o bere, vă rog**
Please may I have the bill	**Nota de plată, vă rog**
coffee	**cafea**
with milk	**cu lapte**
decaffeinated	**făra cafeina**
tea	**ceai**
wine	**vin**
white	**alb**
red	**roşu**
beer	**bere**
draught	**la halbă**
bottled	**la sticlă**
juice	**suc**
orange	**de portocale**
grapefruit	**de grepf**
tomato	**de roşii**
mineral water (sparkling)	**apă plată (minerală)**

HANDY TRAVEL TIPS

An A–Z Summary of Practical Information

A

ACCOMMODATION (see also CAMPING and YOUTH HOSTELS)

Once in Romania, accommodation is likely to be your largest expense, with even very ordinary hotels and guest houses costing more than you would pay in most other countries in Europe. Don't expect service to be all that good either, as it can often leave much to be desired.

In Bucharest at least you'll find a full range of hotels, from the major five-star chain hotels to small boutique hotels, pensions, grotty one-stars and even hostels. An explosion of three-star hotels has recently seen prices fall, but a good room at a busy time of the year will still cost somewhere in the region of €75.

Outside the capital, choice can often be limited to relatively expensive four-star hotels, usually privatised former Communist Party hotels, and smaller bed-and-breakfast-type lodgings. Only the seaside resorts and Poiana Braşov have a full range of hotels. Note that in both cases prices are cheaper if you book a package through an agent, whether in your home country or in Romania. Turning up on spec either at Poiana Braşov or at the seaside can be an expensive experience.

At every railway station in Romania you will be met by a number of old ladies who will offer *cazare* – rooms in their homes. Prices never usually top €10 per night but be warned: while you can often get a real bargain, many homes may not have hot water full-time, and you may be asked to observe a curfew.

I'd like a ...	**Aş vrea...**
single room	**o cameră cu un pat**
double room	**o cameră dublă**
with a bath/shower	**cu baie/cu duş**
What's the rate per day?	**Cât costă pe noapte?**

AIRPORTS

Romania has a number of international airports. The largest is Otopeni Henri Coanda near Bucharest, served by over 30 airlines. The national carrier, Tarom, flies to around 35 destinations worldwide. Otopeni was completely renovated in 2002 and is now a modern, though small, international airport. Getting into the city from Otopeni – some 18km (11 miles) from the city centre – is best done by taxi. Avoid the unofficial taxi drivers who will harass you as you exit the airport, and take one of the well-marked Fly Taxis which line up outside the terminal building. A trip to the city centre should cost no more than 75 lei.

Bucharest has a second, smaller airport, Baneasa, from where the budget airline BlueAir operates flights to Barcelona, Bergamo, Istanbul, Lyon and Maastricht/Aachen. From January 2007, Wizz Air will fly to Baneasa from London Luton. Baneasa is closer to the city centre than Otopeni Henri Coanda: you can take bus No. 385 from outside the terminal to Piaţa Romana.

A number of international flights leave from Timişoara International Airport, including two weekly flights to New York. Cluj-Napoca, Sibiu, Oradea, Arad, Baia Mare, Satu Mare, Iaşi, Suceava and Constanţa also have international airports, though usually with flights only to Italy and Germany, for the benefit of Romanian migrant workers. At these airports – most are some distance from the towns they serve – you should make use of Tarom courtesy buses that serve most flights.

Tarom operates internal flights between Bucharest and all of Romania's airports. These usually cost around €90 return, and are the best way of travelling long distances, as trains are very slow.

B

BICYCLE AND MOTORBIKE HIRE

You can hire mountain bikes in the ski resorts (in Poiana Braşov Club Rossignol has good equipment for hire; tel: 0268-26 24 70 for details), but you will struggle to find anywhere in the cities where you can hire a bike. Cycling is simply not popular.

It's a similar story with motorcycles; motorcycle hire is unheard of in Romania. Indeed, you will rarely see a motorcyclist: the sport has yet to take any kind of root.

BUDGETING FOR YOUR TRIP

Still remarkably cheap by Western European or North American standards, prices in Romania are nevertheless increasing fast. Once you've arrived, accommodation will be your biggest expense.

Transport Travelling around the country by public transport is ludicrously cheap. Even first-class train travel will be within the budget of all but the poorest of travellers. A ticket from Bucharest to Braşov should cost €7–15, depending on the type of train. However, trains are slow and planes are a better, though more expensive option. Single fares from Bucharest to Cluj-Napoca and Sibiu start at around €60.

Within cities, public transport is chaotic but cheap. Taxis are inexpensive, as long as you make sure the taxi is registered. Even a cross-city ride in Bucharest will cost no more than €5–7.

Eating out is as cheap or expensive as you wish. Good cheap cuisine is not difficult to find, but in Bucharest and in the ski resorts especially, you can just as easily spend a fortune. A top-class dinner in one of Bucharest's five-star hotels or flashy restaurants will cost at least €50 per person, but a standard Romanian restaurant will serve hearty portions of local fare for less than €10 per head.

C

CAMPING

Camping is not wildly popular in Romania, and as a result you will not find too many facilities. Romanians prefer making use of the country's vast network of *cabane* – cheap, basic cabins, found mostly in mountain regions, where for a few lei you can get your head down on a bunk and get a simple meal. Don't expect hot water, and toilet facilities will be extremely basic.

Those Romanians who do camp tend to pitch up their tents wherever the mood takes them. Although you can usually do so without worry, make sure you are not on someone's private property.

CAR HIRE (see also DRIVING)

Car hire is expensive, with rates for a medium family saloon starting at around €70 per day. All the major chains have representative offices in Bucharest and a number of other cities, as well as at most airports. Most major hotels can also arrange car hire.

You do not need an international driving licence, as your own standard driving licence is valid in Romania for 90 days. However, Britons should note that the old-style driving licence which does not have a photo must be accompanied by some kind of photographic ID (a passport, for example).

Avis
Bucharest, tel: 021-210 43 45
Otopeni Henri Coanda Airport, tel: 021-201 19 57
Budget
Bucharest, tel: 021-210 28 67
Constanţa, tel: 0241-63 97 13
Timişoara, tel: 0723-05 51 68
Braşov, tel: 0268-47 88 00
Hertz
Bucharest, tel: 021-222 12 56
Otopeni Henri Coanda Airport, tel: 021-201 49 54
Sixt
Bucharest, tel: 021-9400
Otopeni Henri Coanda Airport, tel: 0722-63 23 84

CLOTHING

Winters are cold, summers are hot, so dress accordingly. Spring and autumn tend to be very short. Romanians have few hang-ups about clothing, but you should note that many local women will cover their heads before entering churches and cathedrals, although visitors are under no obligation to do the same. You will also note that Romanians tend to overdress their children horribly: even in high summer you will often see children running around in jumpers and woolly hats.

If invited into a Romanian home you should remove – or at least offer to remove – your footwear. In most cases you will be asked to do so as a matter of course.

CRIME AND SAFETY (see also POLICE)

Romania is a very safe country. Violent crime is almost non-existent, and your most likely source of physical danger will be the wild street dogs that pose a major threat in Bucharest. Pickpockets are common on public transport, especially in railway stations and on buses and trams to and from airports. Backpackers are seen as a particularly good target. The Black Sea's beaches are notorious for thieves.

Aggressive begging on the metro in Bucharest is common, and can be off-putting. Beggars will also approach cars at traffic lights.

My ... has been stolen
    passport/wallet/handbag
Stop thief!
	Mi s-a furat ...
	    paşaport/portofel/poşeta
	Opriţi! Hoţ!

CUSTOMS AND ENTRY REQUIREMENTS

On Romania successfully joining the EU in January 2007, citizens of EU and EEA countries may enter the country without a visa and stay for as long as they wish. Citizens of Moldova, Croatia, the United States, Canada, Australia, New Zealand, Chile and Argentina may also enter visa free for 90 days. Almost everyone else needs a visa.

Visas can no longer be purchased at the border, so must be procured at a Romanian consulate abroad before trying to enter the country. For a full list of countries who are visa-exempt, see the Romanian Foreign Ministry's website <www.mae.ro>. If you wish to extend your stay beyond 90 days, you will need to present yourself at a local police station to obtain an extension. If you stay more than 90 days and then attempt to leave the country without having officially extended your stay, you will be turned back at the border.

Customs regulations are standard, and duty-free allowances pretty much follow international norms: two bottles of alcohol, 200 cigarettes or 50 cigars or 25 grams of tobacco are the personal limits. Cash in excess of €10,000 (or equivalent in any currency) must be declared on entry. On Romania joining the EU in January 2007, there will be no customs or currency restrictions on arrivals from EU countries.

D

DISABLED TRAVELLERS

Romania is making giant strides towards accommodating disabled travellers better, but getting around the country remains difficult for all but the fittest. Sibiu and Timişoara are leading the way, installing rudimentary wheelchair ramps in many public squares, museums and tourist attractions. As a rule, the better the hotel, the more chance of its having facilities for disabled visitors. Bucharest and the Black Sea coast are rich in hotels that would not hesitate in accommodating disabled guests. The mountain resorts are less accessible.

DRIVING (see also CAR HIRE)

Good luck. Romanians drive on the right, though in Bucharest especially almost anything goes. Corrupt local police will happily accept bribes in place of official fines, so there is little to stop local drivers behaving badly on the roads. For what it's worth, the law applies these speed limits: 50kph in built-up areas, 90kph on standard inter-urban roads, 100kph on European roads, and 130kph on motorways.

If you arrive in Romania by car, you will need to show that you have international motor insurance. Your passport will be marked with a small stamp showing you arrived by car. If you then try to leave the country without the car, you will have to explain what happened to it. You will also need to buy an obligatory road-tax disc, called a *rovinieta*, which costs around €20, depending on the length of your stay.

Roads, both in cities and in the countryside, are terrible. There is only one proper motorway, which will eventually run from Bucharest to Constanţa, though currently it only goes about half-way. Most other inter-urban roads are single-lane affairs. You should beware of driving at night, as road surfaces are poor, and few highways have lights. Be especially wary of random Gypsy carts and stray animals when passing through villages. Potholes are ubiquitous.

petrol	**benzină**
diesel	**motorină**
Fill the tank, please.	**Să fie plin, vă rog.**
My car has broken down.	**Masina mi-a în pana.**
Can I park here?	**Pot să staţionez aici?**

E

ELECTRICITY

Romania uses the 200-volt AC system, like much of continental Europe. Visitors from the UK and the US will need a two-pin adaptor for electrical appliances. The power supply these days is good.

EMBASSIES AND CONSULATES

Embassies in Bucharest:
Australia 74 B-dul Unirii, tel: 021-320 98 26.
Canada 36 Str Nicolae Iorga, tel: 021-307 50 00.
Ireland 42–44 Str Vasile Lascăr, tel: 021-212 21 36.
UK 24 Str Jules Michelet, tel: 021-312 03 03.
USA 26 Str Filipescu, tel: 021-210 40 42.

EMERGENCIES (see also POLICE)

For ambulance, police or fire you can call one number throughout the country: **112**. As long as you speak clearly you should be understood. Most operators speak some English and French.

There's been an accident.	**A avut loc un accident**.
Help!	**Ajutor!**
Fire!	**Incendiu!**
Call the …	**Chemaţi …**
police	**poliţia**
ambulance	**salvare**
fire brigade	**pompierii**

G

GAY AND LESBIAN TRAVELLERS

Romania is not particularly freindly towards gays and lesbians. Homosexual activity between consenting adults was only legalised in 2002, and then only after much badgering from the European Union. A poll of young people in late 2005 found that 20 percent of those under 30 still found the practice incomprehensible. Bucharest's annual Gay Pride march, held every June, invariably ends in violence. There are few gay bars and clubs. In many cities there are none at all. For more information, visit the website of Romania's one gay and lesbian organisation, Accept, <www. accept-romania.ro>.

GETTING THERE

Package tours Before 1989 Romania was a cheap favourite of budget skiers in winter, and budget sun-seekers in summer. Today, with prices relatively high, the number of package tourists has decreased, though the authorities are now making efforts to bring them back. If you want to spend a week skiing in Poiana Braşov, a package will be your best option.

Even if you want to travel around the country independently, a package, including a charter flight, transfer and accommodation, can often be your best bet. Poiana Braşov makes a very good base for exploring Southern Transylvania. UK tour operators who fea-ture Romanian ski and beach resorts include Balkan Holidays, <www.balkanholidays.co.uk>.

By air Flying is the best way to reach Romania. There are direct scheduled flights to Bucharest from Amman, Amsterdam, Athens, Beirut, Brussels, Budapest, Chişinau, Damascus, Dubai, Frankfurt, Istanbul, London, Madrid, Milan, Moscow, Munich, New York, Paris, Prague, Rome, Sofia, Tel Aviv, Vienna, Warsaw and Zurich. State airline Tarom still has a monopoly on most routes, and prices remain high. Budget airline BlueAir flies from Bucharest Baneasa to Barcelona, Bergamo, Istanbul, Lyon and Maastricht/Aachen. From January 2007 Wizz Air flies to Bucharest from London Luton.

You can fly to Timişoara direct from Ancona, Bari, Bologna, Florence, Milan, Munich, Rome, Turin, Venice and Vienna. Cluj-Napoca is served by direct flights from Budapest, Munich and Vienna, and Sibiu from Frankfurt, Munich and Vienna. Some charter flights from the UK and Germany serve Constanţa airport during the summer. Contact your travel agent for the best route and price.

By rail You can enter Romania by train from Hungary (coming from Budapest you will cross the border at Curtici, near Arad), Serbia (at Moraviţa, from Belgrade), Bulgaria (at Giurgiu, from Sofia), the Ukraine (at Radauti) and the Republic of Moldova (at Ungheni). There are two daily trains to Bucharest from Sofia, three from Budapest, one from Belgrade, one from Kiev and one from Chişinau.

By road There are numerous road crossings into Romania, from Hungary, Serbia, Bulgaria, the Republic of Moldova and the Ukraine. The busiest, and those most used by Western visitors, are at Nadlac and Bors from Hungary, Moroviţa and Dobreta-Turnu Severin from Serbia, Giurgiu and Vama Veche from Bulgaria, Albita from the Republic of Moldova and Şiret from the Ukraine. Always make sure you have full international motor insurance before trying to cross the border into Romania.

H

HEALTH AND MEDICAL CARE (see also EMERGENCIES)

There are no specific health risks particular to Romania, though you should take out adequate health insurance before travelling. General standards of health care, in urban areas at least, are satisfactory, though in the countryside health care is often very ad hoc. In an emergency call **112** for an ambulance. Emergency medical treatment is free, but you may have to pay for some medicines. You will also be expected to 'tip' doctors and nurses (who are underpaid) very well; otherwise you may receive poor, in some cases non-existent, treatment.

Tap water is safe to drink, though the low cost of the bottled variety means that nobody actually does. Mosquitoes are a problem in most parts of the country during the summer, and insect repellent is a must. Stray dogs are a massive problem in most cities, especially Bucharest. Bites are common, more in summer than winter, and you should be very careful. If you are bitten you will need to have an anti-rabies injection urgently. Incredibly, Romanians seem to enjoy having their cities blighted by this canine plague, and actively help the stray-dog population survive by feeding it. Despite the death of a visiting businessman who was attacked by a stray dog in Bucharest, the authorities have yet to take action.

I need a doctor who speaks English.	**Îmi trebuie un doctor care vorbeşte englezeşte.**
I have been bitten by a stray dog.	**M-a muşcat un maidanez.**
chemist	**farmacie**
dentist	**stomotolog**

HOLIDAYS

Romania has few national holidays. Orthodox Easter is the biggest celebration of all, and usually falls a week or two after Easter in

Western Europe. Note that if a holiday falls on a weekend, so be it. The Western practice of taking the next working day off is not yet a Romanian one.

1 January New Year's Day
April/May Orthodox Easter
1 May Labour Day
1 December National Day (commemorating the union of Transylvania with Wallachia and Moldavia in 1919)
25–26 December Christmas

L

LANGUAGE

Romanian is a Romance language and is spoken by most of the population. Even the Hungarian and German minorities in Transylvania speak some Romanian, if only as a second language. Romanian's written form closely resembles French and Italian, and anyone with knowledge of those should get by. English is increasingly the foreign language of choice among the young, especially in Bucharest and on the Black Sea coast. German will be far more useful in Transylvania.

There are some letters in the Romanian alphabet with no English equivalent:

Ă, ă – prounouced as *er* in fath*er*
Â, â, Î, î – pronounced like the *u* in l*u*ll
Ş, ş – pronounced *sh* as in *sh*eet
Ţ, ţ – pronounced *ts* as in *ts*ar

Note that *î* and *â* are in fact the same letter. Until 1989 only *î* was used, as the authorities attempted to de-Latinise the language. Only the Romanian name of the country – România – was exempted. Indeed, immediately after World War II, when the Soviet Union dominated local politics, even the country's name and language was not exempt, and was written Romînia. Since 1989, both letters have been used (though officially î should only be used when it is at the beginning of a word), and you will see both on street signs.

hello	**bună/salut**
goodbye	**la revedere**
good morning	**bună dimineaţă**
good afternoon	**bună ziuă**
good evening	**bună seară**
good night	**noapte bună**
yes	**da**
no	**nu**
please	**vă rog**
thank you	**mulţumesc**

M

MAPS

Most hotel concierges will be able to provide you with some kind of city or town map, but few are any good. Most are little more than vehicles for local advertisements. One exception is the city guide *Bucharest In Your Pocket*, which has a useful map of central Bucharest inside. Any hotel in Bucharest will have a copy.

An excellent road map of Romania, including maps of every major town centre, is published by Karpatia JIF Szarvas. It can be purchased at most petrol stations and at good bookshops, and costs around 40 lei.

For specialist hiking maps, the tourist information office in Predeal has an excellent selection, and you should also be able to pick up good hiking maps at most good bookstores in Bucharest and Braşov.

Do you have a map of the city?	**Aveţi cumva o hartă a oraşului?**

MEDIA

Local television is poor, though, as with films at the cinema, foreign programmes are shown in their original language with Romanian subtitles. Most hotels offer cable or satellite TV, with a wide variety of foreign news channels. You will find the English press at news-stands in the five-star hotels in Bucharest, including the Hilton and the Marriott, as well as the most centrally located news-stands. You will have to search high and low to find any foreign press outside the capital.

Local English publications are limited to the *Bucharest Daily News*, a rather dry daily newspaper written in questionable English. For restaurant and entertainment listings in the capital, try *Bucharest In Your Pocket*, free at all hotels.

If you can make sense of Romanian, *Şapte Seri (Seven Evenings)* is a free leaflet-sized magazine about local goings-on. It is published weekly in Bucharest and Oradea, and fortnightly in six other major cities. It is written largely in Romanian, with a smattering of English. You will find it in hotels, restaurants and bars. There is also a Romanian version of *Time Out* published bi-weekly in Bucharest.

MONEY

Romania's currency is the leu, plural lei. It is usually written in full *(lei)*. Since July 2005, banknotes have come in denominations of 500, 100, 50, 10, 5 and 1. One leu is subdivided into 100 bani, which come in coins of 50, 20, 10, 5, 2 and 1. You may still find old banknotes in circulation, exactly the same as the new ones though with four extra zeros. These will remain legal tender until the end of 2006, after which they can only be changed in banks.

Where is the nearest bank?	**Unde este bancă cea mai apropiată?**
I want to change …	**Vreau să schimb …**
some money	**nişte bani**
some travellers' cheques	**nişte cecuri de călatori**

Changing money is best done inside a bank. Exchange offices tend to charge exorbitant commissions and/or offer low rates of exchange. ATMs are everywhere, and Visa/MasterCard credit and debit cards are accepted in most hotels, shops and restaurants. Holders of American Express and Diners Club cards may struggle.

Travellers' cheques should always be exchanged in a bank.

O

OPENING HOURS (see also HOLIDAYS)

Government offices, banks and other institutions tend to be open Mon–Fri 8.30am–4pm, usually without a pause for lunch. Most museums are closed Monday, and some also close Sunday. Shops and supermarkets are open Mon–Sat 9am–8pm, though many stay open later. Many shops in major cities now also open on Sunday.

P

POLICE

For police, call **112**. All operators allegedly now speak English, though the police force itself is notoriously monolingual. It is also notoriously corrupt, but you are only liable to encounter a policeman if driving, or if you seek one out for help. Though an attempt has been made to clean up the force, almost any driving offence – especially in the countryside – can still be dealt with by paying a bribe as opposed to a fine. As a foreigner you will be liable to higher bribes. But do not assume you can get out of trouble with a bribe; both drink-driving and excessive speeding are punishable by heavy prison sentences.

You should carry some form of ID with you at all times, as this is law, but random checks are not common. A photocopy of your passport will suffice if you do not wish to carry around the original.

| Where is the police station? | **Unde esta poliția?** |

POST OFFICES

Post offices can be found in even the smallest village, though if you are posting something abroad, it's best do it from Bucharest, otherwise your intended recipient could be kept waiting some time. The central post office in Bucharest is at 10 Str Matei Millo, next to the Carpaţi Hotel, and is open Mon–Fri 7.30am–8pm, and Sat 8am–2pm. You should note, however, that all Romanian post offices are slow, tortuous affairs where getting anything from buying a stamp to sending a parcel can take an age. If you do need to send postcards, it may be worth asking at your hotel if they can take care of buying stamps.

For urgent letters and packets, DHL have offices in most major cities. Call 021-222 17 71 for DHL in Bucharest.

I want to send this by ...	**Aş vrea să trimit această ...**
airmail	**prin avion**
express	**prin poştă rapidă**

PUBLIC TRANSPORT

Taxis The best way to get around any city in Romania is by taxi, though the amount you pay very much depends on what kind of taxi you get into. As long as your cab is clearly marked as belonging to an official company, you should be fine. Legislation in most cities has seen the number of unofficial taxis reduced considerably. But the unknowing visitor can still be ripped off. Be especially careful outside luxury hotels (always ask the concierge to call you a taxi), at airports and at railway stations. Always make sure you know how much you are paying per kilometre: the average amount is between 1 and 1.5 lei per kilometre. All taxis are required to display their tariffs on the side of their cabs.

In Bucharest, trusted taxi companies include Meridian Taxi 021-9444, Taxi Cobalcescu 021-9451 and Cristaxi 021-9461. In Braşov use Martax 0268-313 040 and Rotaxi 0268-319 999, in Timişoara either Gruptaxi 0256-207 207 or Citytaxi 0256-208 686, and in

Constanța and at the coast, Mondial 0241-693 333 or Romarts 0241-690 000.

Please take me to this address	**La adresa aceasta, vă rog**
Please stop here	**Opriți aici, vă rog**

Trains Romania's train service (Calea Ferată Română, CFR) is cheap and efficient, but slow. The Bucharest–Brașov line is very well served, with at least 10 trains a day, the fastest of which (Inter-City) do the journey in just over two hours. The service to Constanța is also good, InterCity trains taking 2½ hours to cover the distance. Travelling any further will cost you almost an entire day: try to use overnight sleeper trains if a long journey is called for.

You can buy tickets for trains at stations from one hour before the train leaves, or further in advance from CFR offices found in the centre of most cities. In Bucharest, the CFR office is at 10–14 Str Domnița Anastasia (Mon–Fri 8am–7.30pm). There are also Wasteels offices selling international railway tickets at Bucharest's Gara de Nord, and at Brașov station.

How much is the fare to …?	**Cât costă pâna …?**
a ticket to …	**un bilet la …**
single (one way)	**doar dus**
return (round trip)	**dus întors**
first/second class	**clasa întaia/a doua**

R

RELIGION

The vast majority of the Romanian population is Romanian Ortho-dox, similar in almost every way to the Orthodoxy practised in Rus-sia, Serbia, Bulgaria and Macedonia. There is a large Hungarian

Catholic minority in Transylvania, as well as a considerable number of Greek Catholics (otherwise Orthodox Christians who recognise the Pope as the head of the Church).

T

TELEPHONE, FAX AND EMAIL

The country code for Romania is +40. The city code for Bucharest is 021, for Braşov 0268. Other important city codes include: Cluj-Napoca 0264, Constanţa 0241, Sibiu 0269, Sinaia 0244 and Timişoara 0256. The first 0 is dropped if calling from abroad. Within Romania, do not use the city code unless you are dialling from outside the city or area. To make an international call from Romania, dial 00.

You can dial internationally from most hotel rooms (though at great cost). All public phones allow direct international dialling. Most news-stands sell phone cards (look out for *Avem cartele Romtelecom*). You can receive or send a fax at a post office.

Internet cafés are everywhere, and cheap to use. Most good hotels also now offer in-room internet access. Romanian internet domains have the suffix <.ro>.

TIME DIFFERENCES

Romania is two hours ahead of Greenwich Mean Time (GMT+2). Clocks go forward one hour on the last Sunday in March, and back again on the last Sunday in October.

New York	London	**Bucharest**	Jo'burg	Sydney	Auckland
5am	10am	**noon**	noon	8pm	10pm

TIPPING

You are expected to tip waiters and waitresses in restaurants (but check your bill to ensure that service is not already included), domestic hotel staff and doormen. In these cases, a 10 percent tip is seen as obligatory, regardless of whether you have been happy with the service. Indeed, the notion of a waiter going out of his way actually to earn a good tip is unheard of.

Unusually, taxi drivers do not expect to be tipped, and you should do so only if you have taken a taxi on a particularly short journey, in order to make the ride worth the driver's time and trouble.

TOILETS

There are very few decent public toilets in Romania. In Bucharest, they're passable in the Unirea, Bucharest Mall and Plaza Romania shopping centres. Those at the Gara de Nord railway station are also just about bearable. In the mountains, even restaurant and mountain-retreat toilets can leave a lot to be desired, and many are of the common squat variety. Bring your own toilet paper.

Where are the toilets?	**Unde e toaleta?**

TOURIST INFORMATION

There are few tourist information offices of any use in Romania. Two notable exceptions are the mountain resort of Predeal, which has an excellent tourist information centre in the forecourt of its railway station, open 10am–4pm daily, and the Transylvanian city of Sibiu, which has a tourist information office on its main square.

Incredibly, in Bucharest, the capital, there is no tourist information office whatsoever.

TOURS AND GUIDES

Most travel agencies throughout Romania can organise tours of specialist sights, including hunting and fishing trips. The Bucharest-based agency Jolly Tour – tel: 021-303 37 96; <www.jollytours.ro> – arranges excellent-value tours of Bucharest and the Carpathian Mountains, and can also arrange private cars with driver and guide for tailor-made trips, starting at around €70 per day. Marshal Turism, also in Bucharest, specialises in hunting, vineyard and monastery tours; tel: 021-319 44 55; <www.marshal.ro>. For tours of the Danube Delta, you should contact Danube Delta Tours; tel: 021-312 25 85; <www.danubedeltatours.ro>.

W

WEBSITES

The best general website is **<www.romaniatravel.com>**, which has good introductions to most Romanian regions and cities, as well as a good photographic database, in a variety of languages. Other good websites include:

<www.daily-news.ro> The website of Romania's only daily English-language newspaper.

<www.inyourpocket.com> Excellent information, restaurant reviews and travel tips for Bucharest, Braşov and Poiana Braşov.

<www.nights.ro> Club and concert listings for most major cities.

<www.psst.ro> A good resource for gossip on Bucharest's restaurants, bars, clubs, the arts and other issues.

<www.romanianjewish.org/en/> An excellent site with news, information and links for Romania's Jewish community and diaspora.

<www.sapteseri.ro> Entertainment listings – in Romanian – for most major Romanian cities.

Y

YOUTH HOSTELS

There are only six hostels in Romania that are affiliated to the Hostelling International Association. Two are in Bucharest (the most famous is the Vila Helga, at 2 Str Salcâmilor, tel: 021-610 22 14), two are in Cluj-Napoca, and there is one in each of Costineşti, Sighişoara and Mangalia. For full details and online bookings take a look at HI's website <www.hihostels.com>.

Recommended Hotels

Good accommodation in Romania is relatively easy to find these days, though it is rarely cheap. There is a wide selection of hotels in Bucharest, in Braşov, at the ski resorts and at the seaside, but the choice in smaller cities and towns is far more limited. In most cases – even five-star hotels – the room rates can often be negotiated, especially at weekends, while for hotels on the coast and in the ski resorts you are far better off booking through a travel agent than turning up on spec. Most hotels at the seaside include an evening meal in their room packages.

The price guides below are for a standard double room, with breakfast, in high season:

€€€	over 200 euros
€€	100–200 euros
€	under 100 euros

BUCHAREST

Athenee Palace Hilton €€€ *1–3 Str Episcopiei, tel: 021-303 37 77, fax: 021-315 21 21, email: <sales.bucharest@hilton.com>, <www.hilton.com>.* The Athenee Palace has been Romania's top hotel since it was built in 1915. Today it is part of the Hilton chain, and offers every possible luxury in a fitting location in Bucharest's most historic square.

Capitol € *29 Calea Victoriei, tel: 021-315 80 30, fax: 021-312 41 69, email: <reservation@hotelcapitol.ro>, <www.hotelcapitol.ro>.* In a good location on historic Calea Victoriei, the Capitol has long been a Bucharest favourite. The hotel was recently renovated and now offers large, well-decorated rooms at reasonable prices.

Crowne Plaza Bucharest €€€ *1 B-dul Poligrafiei, tel: 021-224 00 34, fax: 021-224 11 26, email: <reservations@crowneplaza.ro>,*

<www.bucharest.crowneplaza.com>. If you want Bucharest without the bustle of the city centre itself, this is a good choice. The Crowne Plaza is located in a small park, and comes with large gardens and terraces. The rooms are luxurious.

El Greco €€ *Str Jean Louis Calderon 16, tel: 021-315 81 31/90 00, fax: 021-315 88 98, email:* <office@hotelelgreco.ro>, <www.hotel elgreco.ro>. Four-star hotel in a lovingly restored villa in the old residential heart of Bucharest, just a few hundred metres from Piaţa Universităţii. Rooms are enormous and well furnished, with big double beds and classy bathrooms. There is a superb Greek restaurant on the premises too.

Howard Johnson Grand Plaza €€€ *5–7 Calea Dorobantilor, tel: 021-201 50 00, fax: 021-201 18 88, email:* <sales@hojo plaza.ro>, <www.hojoplaza.ro>. A city-centre high-rise where elegance and charm are never far away. The rooms are large, very well decorated and all at a reasonable price. Bucharest's best Japanese restaurant is inside the hotel.

Intercontinental €€€ *2–4 B-dul Nicolae Bălcescu, tel: 021-310 20 20, fax: 021-312 04 86, email:* <marketing@interconti.com>, <www.intercontinental.com>. One of the city's defining landmarks. Towering over Piaţa Universităţii, the Intercontinental has been welcoming the well-heeled since 1971. The journalists' favourite, you will always find great service accompanying the other luxuries that you would expect from one of the world's leading hotel chains.

J W Marriott €€€ *90 Calea 13 Septembrie, tel: 021-403 10 00, fax: 021-403 10 01, email:* <marriott.bucharest@marriotthotels. com>, <www.marriotthotels.com>. Vast and grandiose, the positively neoclassical façade of the Marriott is one of Bucharest's few modern architectural joys.

Lido €€€ *5–7 B-dul Magheru, tel: 021-314 49 30, fax: 021-312 14 14, email:* <hotel@lido.ro>, <www.lido.ro>. On Bucharest's busiest avenue, the Lido is an art deco masterpiece whose rooms, although they're large and well decorated, are something less than luxurious.

Minerva €€ *2–4 Str Gheorghe Manu, tel: 021-311 15 50, email: <reservation@minerva.ro>, <www.minerva.ro>*. A famous hotel on Bucharest's classiest boulevard, surrounded by fine villas, embassies and apartment blocks. Rooms are perhaps pricey for the size, but the service from all the multilingual staff is exemplary.

Novotel Bucharest City Centre €€ *Calea Victoriei 37B, tel: 021-312 51 14, fax: 021-308 85 00, email: <H5558@accor.com>, <www.novotel.com>*. Brand new, and hiding behind a faux neoclassical façade, this is a comfortable chain hotel in a great location on Calea Victoriei. The swimming pool is one of the largest in the country.

Ramada Majestic €€ *38–40 Calea Victoriei, tel: 021-310 27 72, <www.ramadamajestic.ro>*. A great hotel with a small but quiet indoor swimming pool in the basement. Perfectly located on Calea Victoriei. The rooms are large and little short of luxurious. Pricey.

Rembrandt € *11 Str Smardan, tel: 021-313 93 15, fax: 021-313 93 16, email: <info@rembrandt.ro>, <www.rembrandt.ro>*. A new hotel owned by the same people who run the peerless Amsterdam Grand Café. Rooms here are large, all have antique wooden floors and tasteful furnishings, and there's a trendy night bar too.

Sofitel €€€ *10 Piaţa Montreal, tel: 021-224 30 00, fax: 021-224 25 50, email: <reservations@sofitel.ro>, <www.sofitel.com>*. Modern high-rise opposite Casa Scânteii, part of the World Trade Center. Rooms are luxurious, and those on the upper floors have superb views. There are two first-class restaurants on the ground floor, and guests have free access to the exclusive Le Club, a health club a short courtesy-minibus ride away.

BRASOV

Aro Palace €€€ *9 B-dul Eroilor, tel: 0268-47 88 00, fax: 0268-47 52 28, <www.aro-palace.ro>*. Fully renovated in 2005, this stunning art deco pile is now once again Braşov's best hotel: large rooms with high ceilings and enormous windows have great views across Braşov's central park. The restaurant is a kitsch gem.

Casa Ţepeş € *14 Str Ţepeş, tel/fax: 0268-41 39 17, <www.hotel restaurant.ro/casatepes>*. Great-value rooms in a fine converted house a short walk from the centre of Braşov. We like the loft rooms with the sloping wooden ceilings. There's a kitchen and dining room for guests to use, and a good buffet breakfast is included in the price.

Coroana € *62 Str Republicii, tel: 0268-47 74 48, fax: 0268-41 84 69*. A simple, cheap hotel in central Braşov that has a great deal of charm if not luxury. The building is super, though it has seen better days, and the corridors are a little musty. Rooms are small but all have en-suite facilities, and for the price you'll find nothing more central.

Curtea Braşoveana € *16 Str Bailor, tel: 0268-47 23 36, fax: 0268-47 21 45, <www.curteabrasoveana.ro>*. A number of large, modern and well-equipped rooms and apartments open onto a traditional Transylvanian courtyard in the heart of Braşov's wonderland Schei district. Our favourite accommodation in the city.

Montana Guest House €€ *2A Str Stejaris, tel/fax: 0268-47 27 31, <www.montana.ro>*. A short drive from the city centre on the road to Braşov is the Montana Guest House, a small but lovely villa painted bright green. Views from the large rooms are tremendous, and the breakfast a hearty Transylvanian treat.

POIANA BRASOV

Poiana Braşov is a resort where the streets have no name.

Alpin €€ *tel: 0268-26 23 43, fax: 0268-26 22 11*. For a long time the Alpin *was* Poiana Braşov. It is still the home of the resort's best swimming pool, and the rooms – some of which have been renovated – all have great views of the ski slopes. Note that the cable-cars are a good 15 minutes' walk away.

Casa Vinga €€ *tel/fax: 0268-26 23 34, email: <pensiune@casa vinga.ro>, <www.casavinga.ro>*. Close to the Kanzel cable-car,

Casa Vinga is a small, family-run pension whose pizza restaurant on the ground floor is the resort's best. You can hire skis in winter and mountain bikes in summer.

Club Rossignol € *tel: 0268-26 24 70/47 75 75, fax: 0268-41 74 11.* Large, split-level attic-style rooms with raised sleeping areas above Poiana's liveliest après-ski bar. The Kanzel cable-car is a minute away, and there is ski hire in the basement.

Miruna €€ *tel: 0268-26 21 20/26 24 36, fax: 0268-26 20 35, <www.mirunahotel.ro>.* Quite the best location in Poiana, just behind the Kanzel cable-car and facing the slopes. The terrace is a suntrap, and fills up with sun-worshippers in the afternoon. Rooms have large balconies, enormous bathrooms with hydro-showers and in most cases separate living and sleeping areas.

Poiana €€ *tel: 0268-40 73 30, fax: 0268-40 73 32, <www.ana hotels.ro>.* Good, clean and smart if less than exciting, a hotel aimed squarely at Western package tourists. The après-ski bar on the ground floor is lively most evenings.

Sport €€ *tel: 0268-40 73 30, fax: 0268-40 73 32, <www.ana hotels.ro>.* A larger version of the Poiana *(above)*. Rooms are fine, well appointed and of a good size, but all are more or less the same and the hotel is another package tourist's favourite. Excellent buffet breakfast.

Traveland €€ *tel/fax: 0268-26 24 47, <www.traveland.ro>.* Situated just behind the resort's ice rink, Traveland is a small village of wooden villas, some with two bedrooms, some with four. All have two bathrooms, a living room, fully equipped kitchen and dining area.

SINAIA

International €€ *Str Avram Iancu, tel: 0244-31 38 51, fax: 0244-31 38 55, email: <office@international-sinaia.ro>, <www.inter national-sinaia.ro>.* A large high-rise at the end of Sinaia's main

CONSTANTA

Ibis Constanța €€ *39–41 Str Mircea cel Batran, tel: 0241-50 80 50, <www.accorhotels.com>.* Ibis hotels may not have anything extraordinary to offer, but in Romania that is often a boon. This one is a standard Ibis hotel: a great breakfast complements good service and small but well-equipped rooms.

Royal €€ *191 B-dul Mamaia, tel: 0241-54 55 70, fax: 0241-545882, email: <office@hotelroyal.ro>, <www.hotelroyal.ro>.* Small, elegant hotel in northern Constanța, close to the entrance to Mamaia. Rooms are large and well furnished, all are air conditioned and have great bathrooms. There's a half-decent restaurant too.

MAMAIA

Note: there are no street names in Mamaia.

Bavaria Blu €€ *tel: 0241-83 12 51, fax: 0241-83 14 43, <www.bavariablu.ro>.* A classy hotel at the entrance to Mamaia, well placed for the resort's water park. The Bavaria Blu has large, well-furnished rooms, a good restaurant and a large outdoor swimming pool.

Best Western Savoy €€€ *tel: 0241-83 14 26.* A great hotel with enormous air-conditioned rooms, luxury bathrooms and a great terrace restaurant. It has two outdoor pools (one exclusively for children) and a private beach with water-sports facilities.

Majestic €€ *tel: 0241-83 10 05, fax: 0241-83 19 81, <www.pmg.ro>.* A high-rise with charm and the best buffet breakfast on the coast. It can be a little expensive in high season, but that doesn't seem to stop it being full. Staff are friendly and multilingual.

Rex €€€ *tel: 0241-83 15 95.* Long considered the best hotel on the entire Black Sea coast, the Rex dominates Mamaia beach from its berth in the centre of the resort. Rooms are grand and luxurious, and those with a sea view are utterly romantic. The hotel has its own small private beach.

Recommended Restaurants

Although Romanian cuisine itself is less than inventive, it will be a relief to know that the country's restaurants are as good as any in Central and Eastern Europe. Bucharest even has a couple of restaurants to rival the world's best. As a rule, eating out remains relatively inexpensive, but prices are increasing fast. You will keep the cost down by drinking local wine, as imported wines are expensive. When ordering in seafood restaurants, always find out if the price shown on the menu relates to an individual serving or to 100 grams of fish. And beware of waiters who offer to bring you a selection of local delicacies without telling you the price. This practice goes on even at the best Romanian restaurants.

The price guides below are for a three-course meal, per person, not including drinks:

€€€	over 20 euros
€€	10–20 euros
€	under 10 euros

BUCHAREST

Amsterdam Grand Café €€ *6 Str Covaci, tel: 021-313 75 80, <www.amsterdam.ro>*. A wonderful café, bar and restaurant where excellent international food is served all day. There's a lively club in the basement on Friday and Saturday nights too.

Balthazar €€€ *2 Str Dumbrava Roşie, tel: 021-212 14 60, fax: 021-212 14 61, <www.balthazar.ro>*. Join Bucharest's smart set at the city's best restaurant. An original fusion menu is complemented by an outstanding wine list. You'll need a reservation at the weekend.

Barka Saffron €€€ *1 Str Av. Sănătescu, tel: 021-224 10 04*. Laidback, smart and uber-trendy Indian restaurant popular with media types who work in the surrounding villas and offices. A great place for evening cocktails.

Benihana €€€ *5–7 Calea Dorobantilor (Howard Johnson Hotel), tel: 021-201 50 30, <www.benihana.ro>.* A superb but outrageously expensive Japanese restaurant, the only one in Romania worth eating at. The food is cooked before your eyes on *tepanyaki* grills.

Bistro Atheneu € *3 Str Episcopiei, tel: 021-313 49 00.* A charming olde-worlde atmosphere oozes through the wooden dining rooms at this Bucharest institution. Chose your dish from the daily specials marked up on the blackboard.

Casa di David Downtown €€€ *56 Str Lascar Catargiu, tel: 021-317 45 51.* Modern Italian food in a sublime setting just off Piața Victoriei. There is a large trendy terrace in summer, while the inside dining rooms are equally splendid, with enormous high ceilings.

Café Royal Brasserie €€ *1–3 Str Episcopiei (Hilton Hotel), tel: 021-303 37 77.* The Hilton's coffee shop is where the smart set meet for lunch and early evening drinks. Great breakfasts, good-value burgers and light bistro food.

Die Deutsche Kneipe € *9 Str Stockholm, tel: 0722-284 560.* A fantastic tiny little *kneipe* owned and run by a cheerful German couple who serve massive portions of German sausage, pork knuckle and sauerkraut. Don't forget to leave room for apfelstrudel desserts, too. Reservations essential. Closed on Sundays.

Kiraly Csarda €€ *177 Calea Dorobantilor, tel: 021-230 40 83, fax: 021-230 42 03, <www.kiralycsarda.ro>.* Tremendous Transylvanian and Hungarian cuisine is served in massive portions at this fine restaurant, set in a large airy villa in Bucharest's finest residential area.

La Taifas € *16 Str Gh. Manu, tel: 021-212 77 88.* A long-time favourite of Bucharest's chattering classes, where great Romanian food is served for almost nothing. Its eternal popularity makes reservations a must.

Mesogios €€€ *49 Str Calderon, tel: 021-313 49 51/650 03 44, <www.mesogios.ro>*. This is Bucharest's best seafood restaurant. All the fish is flown in fresh daily from Greece, ensuring high quality and high prices.

Moods €€ *63 Str Petre Creţu, tel: 021-224 68 51, <www.moods lounge.com>*. An eclectic restaurant where the menu is modern Thai with a European twist. You'll love the relaxed atmosphere, and the sublime terrace and garden out back in summer.

Taverna Sarbului €€€ *31 Str Tipografilor, tel: 021-490 60 50, fax: 021-490 60 52, <www.tavernasarbului.ro>*. Tasty Serb specialities are served by pretty waitresses in fetching costumes to large groups of friends who flock to the informal atmosphere offered by this often boisterous restaurant.

Trattoria Il Calcio €€ *14 Str Mendeleev, tel: 0722-134 299*. An amiable Italian restaurant in the centre of the city where the tables are so close together you can't help striking up conversation with the people next to you. The food is terrific and reasonably priced. Murals of football stars adorn the walls and all the waitresses wear football strips.

Uptown Bar & Grill €€€ *2 Str Rabat, tel: 021-231 40 77*. A classy villa with a covered terrace that attracts the cream of Bucharest society. The food can be patchy in quality at times, but the ambience more than makes up for that. Reservations essential.

BRASOV

Blue Corner €€€ *3 Piaţa George Enescu, tel: 0268-47 85 90*. An enchanting French restaurant owned by a jovial Romanian chef who makes a point of meeting all his customers if time allows. Come for lunch and end up spending the entire afternoon and evening here.

Butoiul Sasului € *53–55 Str Republicii, tel: 0268-41 04 99.* Enjoy Saxon, Transylvanian and Hungarian specialities for knock-down prices in this popular cellar restaurant off Braşov's main street.

Deane's Irish Pub & Grill €€€ *9 Str Republicii, tel: 0268-41 17 67/0744-18 55 53, <www.deanes.ro>.* An imaginative menu of traditional Irish and modern British dishes are served up in a large cellar pub and restaurant by lovely staff. If Haydn, the owner, is around, he'll make a point of introducing himself, and in the evenings he often takes the microphone and gives his patrons a song.

Gaijin Bar €€€ *27 Piaţa Sfatului, tel: 0268-47 24 61.* Aromatic Thai food in an aromatic Thai setting in an alley just north of Piaţa Sfatului. The smell of burning joss sticks will beckon you down a spiral staircase to an underground dining room where reasonably authentic Thai food awaits.

Taverna €€€ *6 Str Politehnicii, tel: 0268-47 46 18.* Long regarded as Braşov's best restaurant, Taverna is the home of imaginative Romanian food, where a modern twist is placed on traditional favourites. You'll need a reservation most evenings.

POIANA BRASOV

Coliba Haiducilor €€ *tel: 0268-26 21 37.* Romania's most famous restaurant, and a real treasure. Traditional Romanian countryside and hunting dishes are served with gallons of wine, *ţuică* and bonhomie, while a Gypsy *taraf* goes from table to table, fiddling away. You'll need a reservation.

Vânatorul €€€ *tel: 0268-26 23 54.* An elegant restaurant with a sensational terrace serving fine game dishes for high prices. If you want to try a bear steak, this is the place to come.

SINAIA

Cabana Schiorilor € *7 Drumul Cotei, tel: 0244-31 36 55, fax: 0244-31 50 25, <www.cabanaschiorilor.ro>.* Cheap and cheerful it may be, but the terrace, which overlooks the old wooden Sinaia bobsleigh run (no longer used), is a great place to enjoy good Romanian fare in the crisp mountain air.

Taverna Sarbului €€ *Calea Codrului, tel: 0244-31 44 00, fax: 0244-31 43 48, <www.tavernasarbului.ro>*. The Serb specialities come thick and fast here, and in enormous portions. Prices are relatively cheap, and the big wooden tables are usually full of hungry après-skiers and hikers filling up with tasty food and big glasses of beer.

SIBIU

Gasthof Clara €€ *24 Str Raului, tel: 0269-22 29 14, fax: 0269-22 40 03*. Enjoy tasty, hearty Saxon specialities in charming surroundings, served by friendly, bubbly waitresses in starched pinafores. There aren't many tables in this hotel restaurant, so you will need a reservation.

La Turn €€ *1 Piaţa Mare, tel: 0269-21 39 85*. An eternally popular restaurant and terrace in the centre of Sibiu's main square. The food is traditional Romanian, with *ciorbe* (sour soups) a speciality. If you don't want to eat, you are free to sit on the terrace and simply enjoy a beer.

Sibiu Vechi €€ *3 Str Papiu Ilarian, tel: 0269-43 19 71*. A famous Romanian cellar restaurant serving Transylvanian dishes in huge portions. Staff are dressed in traditional costume, and make eating here a real pleasure. Great value.

SIGHISOARA

Casa Vlad Dracul €€€ *5 Str Cositorarilor, tel: 0744-518 108*. It may seem strange taking lunch or dinner at the birthplace of Vlad Dracul, but that doesn't stop coachloads of tourists from flocking here every day. The food is rather good, traditional Romanian fare, but can be expensive. It is advisable to phone ahead for a reservation.

CLUJ-NAPOCA

Agape €/€€€ *6 Str Iuliu Maniu, tel: 0264-40 65 23*. With a great location just off Piaţa Unirii, Agape is a restaurant in two parts: there's a self-service fast-food place at the front, and a classier, more expensive restaurant at the back. Both are recommended, for either a quick lunch or a formal dinner.

Matei Corvin €€€ *3 Str Matei Corvin, tel: 0264-59 74 96*. An upmarket Transylvanian restaurant which is the default choice of visiting businessmen keen to sample local specialities. The atmosphere can be stuffy and prices are high, but the food is super.

Noblesse €€€ *12 Str Ioan Ratiu, tel/fax: 0264-59 24 64, 0722-63 81 19*, *<www.restaurantnoblesse.ro>*. One block west of Piaţa Unirii is this modern restaurant, where traditional Romanian meets modern European and fuses to form a delightfully eclectic menu. The covered terrace room is a cooling spot in high summer, while the more traditional dining rooms ooze class and style.

Roata €€ *6 Str Alexandru Ciura, tel: 0264-59 02 22*. A famous Romanian and Transylvanian restaurant on a dead-end street a short walk from Piaţa Unirii. The smallish garden is usually full on summer evenings, and regardless of the heat everyone appears to order steaming bowls of home-made *ciorba*.

TIMISOARA

Camelot €€ *2 Str Barbu Iscovescu, tel: 0256-22 11 87*, *<www.camelot.ro>*. Feel like a medieval king as serving wenches bring you wooden platters of meat, game and vegetables. You'll find it on the east bank of the Bega behind the Vasile Parvan park.

Casa cu Flori €€ *1 Str Alba Iulia, tel: 0256-43 05 80*. This is the place to come for good, traditional Romanian and Banat specialities. A small terrace fills up quickly in summer, as punters enjoy well-priced food and drinks.

Lloyd €€€ *2 Piaţa Victoriei, tel: 0256-29 49 49.* Though the grandeur of this elegant restaurant has faded slightly over the years, it is still the smartest in Timişoara. The international menu is extensive, the food can often be excellent, and the terrace, out on Piaţa Victoriei, is great for people-watching.

Taco Loco €€€ *9 Spl Tudor Vladimirescu, tel: 0256-20 43 33.* Down on the Bega riverfront, Taco Loco serves more than 50 different Tex-Mex dishes in a lively, modern setting. Reasonably authentic food, but the prices are a bit steep.

IASI

Little Texas €€ *31 Strada Moara de Vant (Little Texas Hotel), tel: 0232-27 25 45, fax: 0232-27 25 45, <www.littletexas.org>.* Outstanding Tex-Mex food in eastern Romania brought to you by Jerry Little, an American who settled with his family in Iaşi years ago. House specialities include marinated sizzling beef fajitas, hand-rolled tortilla chips and deep-dish double-crust apple pie.

CONSTANŢA

El Greco €€ *18 Str Decebal, tel 0722-41 40 10.* A splendid and authentic Greek restaurant in downtown Constanţa. The classical Greek decor may be a bit over the top for some, but the food, including hundreds of *meze*, kebabs, seafood dishes and even lamb, will make your meal here memorable.

Irish Pub €€ *1 Str Ştefan cel Mare, tel 0241-55 04 00, <www. irishpub.ro>.* Sometimes only bacon and eggs will do. In fact, the menu here is surprisingly extensive, and the food good. The terrace is one of the most popular in the city and, yes, they have draught Guinness.

On Plonge € *Portul Turistic Tomis, tel: 0241-60 19 05.* It's the location you'll come for, out on a quay overlooking a quiet section of Constanţa harbour. The food is a little unimaginative, standard Romanian fish dishes such as carp, trout and pike-perch.

INDEX